No Simple Solutions

No Simple Solutions

Transforming Public Housing in Chicago

Susan J. Popkin

COPUBLISHED
WITH THE URBAN INSTITUTE PRESS

ROWMAN & LITTLEFIELD
Lanham • Boulder • New York • London

Copublished with the Urban Institute Press

Urban Institute Editorial Advisory Board
Bridget Lowell, vice president for strategic communications and outreach
Margery Austin Turner, senior vice president for program planning and management
John Rogers, executive vice president, treasurer, and chief financial officer
Scott Forrey, editorial consultant

Published by Rowman & Littlefield
A wholly owned subsidiary of The Rowman & Littlefield Publishing Group, Inc.
4501 Forbes Boulevard, Suite 200, Lanham, Maryland 20706
www.rowman.com

Unit A, Whitacre Mews, 26-34 Stannary Street, London SE11 4AB

Copyright © 2016 by Rowman & Littlefield

British Library Cataloguing in Publication Information Available

Library of Congress Cataloging-in-Publication Data Is Available
ISBN 978-1-4422-6882-1 (cloth : alk. paper)
ISBN 978-1-4422-6883-8 (electronic)

♾™ The paper used in this publication meets the minimum requirements of American National Standard for Information Sciences—Permanence of Paper for Printed Library Materials, ANSI/NISO Z39.48-1992.

Printed in the United States of America

Contents

Foreword

In the 1980s and 1990s, public housing was on trial in Chicago. William Julius Wilson had released the blockbuster book *The Truly Disadvantaged* (1987), arguing that the War on Poverty had been lost due to discriminatory policies that locked the black poor into neighborhoods that were increasingly isolated from jobs and the middle class. Too often, the U.S. Department of Housing and Urban Development's (HUD) Chicago Housing Authority (CHA) was the landlord. Douglas Massey and Nancy Denton, authors of the landmark work *American Apartheid*[1] used Chicago to illustrate how housing policy was a profound force in perpetuating racial segregation. Named plaintiff Dorothy Gautreaux's lawyers had argued as much when she and other CHA residents brought a series of class action suits against HUD and the CHA beginning in 1966, charging that the housing authority had deliberately segregated African-American families through its tenant selection and site selection policies. The case went to the Supreme Court, and Gautreaux won.[2]

My first encounter with the CHA was in 1982, when a college internship landed me in the environs of the notorious Cabrini-Green, arguably the project with the worst reputation in the nation. Just before I had moved to Chicago as a college freshman, Mayor Jane Byrne had moved into Cabrini in an effort to fight violence. By the time I had graduated from college and started graduate school, I was spending much of my time in Cabrini, the Robert Taylor, Stateway Gardens, Ida B. Wells, and other CHA's storied complexes, conducting research for my first book, *Making Ends Meet* (with Laura Lein).[3]

On my first visit to the Henry Horner Homes, several young men mistook my black puffy jacket as a uniform and yelled "Cops!" as I entered the foyer. Someone hit the breaker, leaving a couple dozen residents, plus me, standing in the darkness between the mailboxes and the elevators. Three friendly female faces were soon illuminated by lighters, each eager to assist me in getting to where I needed to go. Once I got to the 14th floor, I met the broken middle-aged woman I had come to interview. She claimed she was so afraid of the gangs that she hadn't left her unit in over a decade. While we talked, her young adult son stood at the door like a sentinel, with a gun-sized bulge in the pocket of his hoodie. It was only when I got to my car that I began crying, shaken by the encounter.

These experiences, though, were only a tiny taste of the trauma that many of these families had suffered, due to the social isolation, the physical degradation, and the violence of their addresses.

In the early 1990s, about five years before the Plan for Transformation would be unveiled, I met an unkempt mother with 10 kids living in the Ogden Arms. There was plywood over the windows because gunfire had shattered the large picture window pane several nights before, gaps letting in a brutal winter cold. She confided that the youngest seven kids were the progeny of a drug dealer. When he stopped by, he wore an expensive track suit. In and out of the back room and back out of the apartment door, he paid no mind to the kids. The younger ones had gone nearly a full day without a diaper change to conserve on Pampers, their disposables so full of liquid that they threatened to drag on the floor. The first three children, however, were the result of incest. Chillingly, the perpetrator, her father, was now living in one of the unit's back bedrooms.

Daughter Ruby, at three, was a charmer on that first visit, climbing on my lap, playing with the tape recorder, interrupting the conversation by assuming cute poses or offering exuberant hugs. Yet two days later, when I returned with small presents for Ruby and the other kids, she showed no sign of recognition. Expressionless, she remained sitting on the floor inert while her siblings played with their new toys.

By the mid-1990s, virtually everyone agreed that something had to be done, so the Plan for Transformation was born, a monumental effort that would change the fabric of Chicago—particularly its south and west sides, profoundly, for better or ill.

No Simple Solutions is both epic and encyclopedic in its up-close chronicle of the Plan for Transformation, the politics that surrounded it, the institutional players who guided it, and those who provided the research infrastructure to evaluate it and hold the CHA accountable. More than that, it reveals the human drama unleased by the transformation. Like me, Susan Popkin had spent years talking to CHA residents, documenting the monumental failure of the agency's—and the City's—efforts to control the gang violence and drug trafficking that overwhelmed their communities and dominated their lives (*The Hidden War*).[4] With the decision to move forward with the Plan, Popkin wanted to know what would happen to the residents whose housing was slated to be demolished or reborn as mixed-income housing. As the towers came down, Popkin devised longitudinal surveys. She also insisted on up-close interviews with both parents and children, determined to put skin on the numbers in an effort to truly measure the human gains and costs.

The book asks and answers the hard questions about the Plan. Were residents actually better off after the transformation? Did the gains to the adults extend to the kids? If not, what would be required to make it so? And why were the boys particularly vulnerable and what kind of interventions would they need to succeed? Was it true that relocation at such a huge scale released a crime wave in those places to which families moved, as alleged in a viral essay in *The Atlantic*, by Hanna Rosin? How about in the areas they left behind, and for the city as a whole?[5]

Susan Popkin spent more than two decades becoming intimately familiar with the contours of a housing authority that was then called the nation's worst. She explored each of the vast array of complexes under the CHA's command and their surrounding environs firsthand, before, during, and after the Plan for Transformation. As the drama of the Plan unfolded, she asked new questions, found new partners, and deployed new research. Finally, she found ways to partner with nonprofits and civic partners to intervene where her work indicated vulnerability or harm. These interventions were then subjected to the same level of scrutiny as she'd directed at the CHA itself.

No Simple Solutions is an honest book about a complex policy that had winners and losers and involved tough trade-offs. It is a smart book, bringing the best of what we can learn from surveys together with in-depth, on-the-ground qualitative work. It is a book that chronicles, along the way, the remarkable career of a remarkable researcher who has dedicated herself to improving the lives of those families she has followed for more than two decades. Ultimately, it is a hopeful book, which gives credit where it is due. Well written, with a compelling narrative arch, it is an absolutely necessary book for anyone who cares about how we house the poor.

Kathryn Edin
Bloomberg Distinguished Professor, Department of Sociology,
Johns Hopkins University

NOTES

1. Douglas S. Massey and Nancy A. Denton. 1998. *American Apartheid: Segregation and the Making of the Underclass*. Cambridge, MA: Harvard University Press.

2. Arnold Hirsch. 1983. *Making the Second Ghetto: Race and Housing in Chicago, 1940–1960*. Chicago: University of Chicago Press.

3. Kathryn Edin and Laura Lein. 1997. *Making Ends Meet: How Single Mothers Survive Welfare and Low-Wage Work.* New York: Russell Sage Foundation.

4. Susan J. Popkin, Victoria E. Gwiasda, Dennis P. Rosenbaum, Lynn M. Olson, and F. Larry Buron. 2000. *The Hidden War: Crime and the Tragedy of Public Housing in Chicago.* New Brunswick, NJ: Rutgers University Press.

5. Hanna Rosin. 2008. "American Murder Mystery." *The Atlantic Monthly* 301(1): 40–54.

Acknowledgments

Following the CHA and its families has shaped my life and career in ways I never could have imagined when I first set foot in the Robert Taylor Homes in 1986. I am heartened that I have had the opportunity to continue this work long enough to see the CHA emerge from its darkest days, and saddened that even all of the changes have done so little to shape the life chances of the children who live in its housing. My first and biggest thanks must go to the many CHA residents who have so generously shared their time, their stories, and their insights with me over the years.

The Urban Institute has been my professional home for 18 years and has provided enthusiastic support for my work on the CHA. I could not have done this work without the contributions of many current and former colleagues who helped keep the projects moving forward and contributed their energy, insights, and ideas. I am especially grateful to my colleague and friend Marge Turner for recognizing the importance of my work on CHA and cheering me on since I arrived at the Urban Institute in 1998. I thank Rolf Pendall for pushing me to write this book and to make it truly my story, not just another research report. Scott Forrey of the Urban Institute Press enthusiastically supported that concept and saw me through a long and frequently disrupted writing process. Jeaneen Zanovello jumped in at the end to help me get the manuscript to the finish line. I am grateful to Jon Sisk and his team at Rowman & Littlefield for making this book the first to appear under the new Urban Institute Press imprint.

Many current and former colleagues worked on interviews, analysis, and reports for the different studies, all generous with their ideas, enthusiasm, and insights. Megan Gallagher, Mary Cunningham, Diane Levy, and Laura Harris all had leadership roles on the HOPE VI Panel Study; Megan also directed the Long-Term Outcomes project in 2011, and Mary was my collaborator on our research on the early phases of the Plan and the original Hard to House project. My former colleague and dear friend Robin Smith worked on the Panel Study research and led the first phase of the teens and food insecurity work. Elsa Falkenburger has been my partner and right-hand woman for all aspects of the HOST Demonstration and Brett Theodos led the research for the Chicago Family Case Management Demonstration. Thanks to Chantal Hailey, Reed Jordan, Joe Parilla, Chris Hayes, Leah Hendey, Molly Scott, Marla McDaniel, Priya Saxena, Sade Adeeyo, Martha Galvez, and the many others who contributed to these complex projects over the years. Special thanks to my colleagues outside the Urban Institute, George Galster, Wes Skogan, and Michael Rich, for their contributions to the Public Housing and Crime research; Isabel Farrar of the University of Illinois Survey Research Lab; and especially, my long-time friend Larry Buron of Abt Associates, who began working with me on the project on crime in CHA developments in 1996 and continued all the way through the end of the Long-Term outcomes project in 2013.

A special thanks to my friend and old graduate school buddy Kathy Edin for her wonderful foreword and for her work to call attention to the plight of poor Americans.

This book draws on multiple research projects carried out over my 18 years at the Urban Institute, and I owe thanks to many funders who have supported my work. Of course, the opinions reflected here are my own and may not reflect those of my funders or of the Urban Institute. My first and biggest thanks go to the MacArthur Foundation, which provided funding for the writing of this book (including the additional interviews with key actors involved in the Plan), as well as major funding for the CHA/HOPE VI Panel Study, the Chicago Family Case Management Demonstration, the Public Housing Transformation and Crime project, and the CHA Relocation Study, all as part of its investment in the Plan for Transformation. I am grateful to Julia Stasch and her team—especially Erika Poethig (now my colleague at the Urban Institute), and Ianna Kachoris, Herman Brewer, Alaina Harkness, Craig Howard, and Susan Lloyd—for investing in me, providing moral support along the way, and hosting many wonderful release events. The Department of Housing and Urban Development provided the initial funding for the HOPE VI Panel Study and support for the HOST Demonstration under grant numbers RP-12-DC-002 and RP-15-DC-001. Special thanks to Ron Ashford, Garland Allen (now retired), Todd Richardson, and Mark Shroder for their insights and interest in this work. The Annie E. Casey Foundation also provided major support for the HOPE VI Panel Study, the Chicago Family Case Management, and HOST. Thanks to Cindy Guy and Charles Rutheiser for their insights and support for this body of work. Special thanks to Mimi Corcoran and Shelley Waters-Boots of the Open Society Foundations for believing in me and allowing me to create the HOST Demonstration. The Rockefeller Foundation provided critical funding for the Chicago Family Case Management Demonstration; thanks to Darren Walker, now President of the Ford Foundation, for believing me and in the work. The Kresge, Kellogg, and Paul Allen Foundations all provided substantial support for the HOST Demonstration. The Ford Foundation funded the Residents at Risk study, described in Chapter 4. The Chicago Community Trust and the Partnership for New Communities both provided funds for the Case Management Demonstration, and the Fannie Mae Foundation provided funds for the HOPE VI Panel Study. Finally, a special thanks to my funders and research partners at Feeding America, Monica Hake, Shaina Alford, and Elaine Waxman (now my colleague at the Urban Institute), and to my friend and former coauthor Xavier de Souza Briggs at the Ford Foundation for supporting the work on teens and food insecurity discussed in Chapter 5.

Last, but not least, I owe a huge debt of thanks to the Chicago Housing Authority, which funded the Chicago Family Case Management Demonstration, HOST, and the Public Housing and Crime Study. I am grateful that I have gotten to know so many amazing and dedicated staff along the way and am especially grateful to Dr. Mary Howard, the CHA's Chief Resident Services Officer, whom I'm honored to be able to call my collaborator and my friend. I am thankful to her and her colleagues for all of their support and for tolerating being the subjects of my research for so long. Special thanks also to current and former CHA staffers Kellie O'Connell Miller, Andy Teitelman, Lewis Jordan, and Linda Kaiser. I also thank my colleagues at HomeForward, the housing authority of Portland and Multnomah County, and the DC Housing Authority for the many contributions they have made to HOST. Special thanks to John Keating and Rachel Langford in Portland and Adrianne Todman, Executive Director of the DCHA.

I express deep thanks and admiration to all of the dedicated people who worked for the social service agencies involved in both the Chicago Family Case Management Demonstration and HOST: Heartland Alliance, Housing Choice Partners, UCAN, Project Match, SGA, and Youth Guidance. The work they do is hard and often overwhelming; their dedication to CHA's families is inspiring. I am especially grateful to all of the staff for putting up with the demands that came with being part of research demonstrations, including participating in regular calls and site visits, tolerating endless requests for data, and for offering their insights in many rounds of interviews and focus groups. I owe a special debt to Kyle Higgins (formerly of UCAN) for allowing me to use some of his beautiful and sad photographs of the last days of Cabrini-Green. I also offer a special thanks to Alex Polikoff, Hoy McConnell, and Julie Brown of BPI for always being willing to talk to me about what was going on at the CHA and for their years of dedication to helping CHA families.

Finally, the past 10 years have been an extremely difficult time for me and my family, with too many painful losses and serious illnesses. I could not have made it through this journey without the support of my family, friends, and colleagues—too many to name here. But I especially thank Julia Keiter-Gaspar and Judy Deane for long walks, cups of tea, and always being willing to listen. I also want to thank my children, Zachary and Rachel Popkin-Hall, and my nephew, now son, Damian Popkin, for providing so much joy and distraction and for putting up with my leaving them so often to travel to Chicago. And most of all, I thank Norm Hall, my husband and partner for 36 years and the love of my life. The caregivers among us often do not get the recognition they deserve, and I could not do the work I do without all of the sacrifices he has made to care for me, our children, and my mother. This book is dedicated to him.

Chapter One

Transforming Public Housing, Changing Residents' Lives

For more than 40 years, Chicago's enormous public housing high-rises dominated the city's poorest African-American neighborhoods, bringing crime and drug trafficking and blighting the lives of the families that lived in them. But 15 years ago, the City of Chicago began a remarkable odyssey that would help the Chicago Housing Authority (CHA) evolve from the most dysfunctional public landlord in America to the ordinary city bureaucracy it is today. The CHA's Plan for Transformation called for demolishing all 11 of the agency's notorious high-rise family developments and replacing them with new, state-of-the-art mixed-income communities, as well as rehabilitating thousands of units in senior buildings and smaller family properties.[1] The Plan is still not complete, and the CHA and the City are still debating final decisions about the fate of the remaining public housing, so it is still too early to make a final assessment how successful it has been in achieving its ambitious goals. But there is no question that its transformation has changed the face of the city—and that it has profoundly changed the lives of the thousands of families that lived in these developments.

TRANSFORMING THE CHA

The effort to transform the CHA was big, messy, and, being a Chicago story, highly politicized. Then-Mayor Richard M. Daley played a central role, putting his considerable political muscle behind the Plan and ensuring that there was enough money to proceed.[2] The CHA's Central Advisory Council (CAC), its agency-wide resident organization, also played a key role, negotiating a formal Relocation Rights Contract—and then litigating to enforce it. Other core players included the U.S. Department of Housing

1

and Urban Development (HUD), the Chicago-based MacArthur Foundation, lawyers, social service agencies, and a host of advocates, journalists, and researchers—including me.

Others have written about the CHA's transformation and have offered critiques of the effort, including its effects on affordable housing in Chicago and the limitations of the shift to mixed-income housing.[3] But to me, the core of the CHA's transformation is the story of what happened to the residents. Before the Plan for Transformation began, the CHA's portfolio of aging, high-crime developments was the worst of public housing in the nation, and its residents lived in fear and squalor. During the 1980s and 1990s, reformers and local government officials tried repeatedly—and unsuccessfully—to fix the housing authority's management problems, improve maintenance, and elimin-ate the drug trafficking and gang violence. Some of these attempts were essen-tially public relations efforts, like then-Mayor Jane Byrne's temporary move into a Cabrini-Green high-rise, while others involved concerted—and costly—initiatives intended to "sweep out" crime and improve security.[4] Still, condi-tions for CHA families steadily deteriorated until 1995, when the HUD finally took over the agency, setting the stage for the large-scale transformation.

The CHA's Plan incorporated some of the lofty goals of federal HOPE VI program, which funded the transformation of public housing nationwide: it aimed to provide residents with an improved living environment and help them move from poverty toward self-sufficiency.[5] Given Chicago's history of combative politics, it is no surprise that different actors have strong opin-ions about whether the residents were treated fairly, if the Plan was merely another iteration of urban renewal, and how well the CHA actually met its obligations for relocation and resident services. The purpose of this book is to bring together evidence to this debate, drawn from primarily two rigorous Urban Institute studies that I have led over the past 15 years.

For nearly 30 years, I have been doing research that focuses on the lives of CHA's residents and how they have experienced the many policy interven-tions and changes that have aimed to improve their lot. I began talking to CHA families when I was a 25-year-old graduate student and have been fol-lowing the path of the CHA and its families ever since. In this book, I tell the story of what happened to families as a result of the Plan for Transformation through the lens of a long-time observer of the CHA and its travails. The research I draw on for this book followed the experiences of hundreds of CHA families as they lived through massive public housing transformation, from the earliest stages in 2001 through to 2013. These families came from two of CHA's lesser-known communities—the Madden/Wells complex and the Dearborn Homes—and some had originally lived in other, more notorious developments, including the Robert Taylor Homes. Many of these families have fared surprisingly well, but others are still struggling, and there are worrying signs that the transformation and relocation was particularly difficult for adolescents. And given that these are deeply poor families who endured years of trauma and stress in CHA's urban war zones, even those who have fared the best are still dealing with enormous, complex challenges.

I start by introducing three families whose experiences illustrate the different paths CHA households followed as they experienced the massive upheaval that resulted from the Plan for Transformation. All were lifelong CHA residents, and all struggled in different ways with the challenges of relocating from their long-term homes and navigating new housing situations and communities. Michelle and her daughter followed the most positive path—although they stayed in Wells long after conditions there became almost intolerable, they ultimately ended up in an apartment Oakwood Shores, the mixed-income community that replaced it, both employed and both relatively content. Matthew and his grandchildren also stayed in Wells until the end, but their path was much bumpier. They tried to move to Oakwood Shores but could not meet the work requirement and ultimately ended up moving to a smaller CHA development, where they, too, were comfortable. Finally, Annette and her children moved out of CHA housing altogether, choosing to relocate with a Housing Choice Voucher that paid their rent for a private-market apartment.[6] Annette already had serious problems before she left Wells—a history of drug addiction, violence, and rocky relationships—and she and her children struggled even more once they left public housing.

The CHA's Plan for Transformation not just supposed to replace its dilapidated housing but also help the very poor families that lived in its developments move towards self-sufficiency and, ultimately, a better life. But by design, the Plan brought more problems—involuntary relocation—to families already struggling to cope with unstable situations—financial stress, short-term jobs, health problems, family members in and out of the criminal justice system, and domestic violence.[7] Together these three stories highlight the potential and limitations of a using a housing-only solution to the many challenges facing vulnerable low-income families and the need for wrap-around supports to protect children and help parents improve their circumstances—themes I will return to throughout this book.

MICHELLE AND TONYA—MAKING A LIFE IN MIXED-INCOME HOUSING

Michelle is one of the residents who have fared relatively well. It is arguable whether her life has been truly "transformed," but she is living in a new mixed-income development and is steadily employed. A long-time resident of the Ida B. Wells Homes, she started from a better position than many of her peers. Although she was a single mother of four children and grew up in CHA housing, she graduated from high school and attended college. She and her children were generally healthy and strong. And unlike many of her neighbors, she never fully disconnected from the labor market, but rather cycled in and out of low-wage jobs. With her relative advantages, she was able to successfully navigate the years of disruption, steadily deteriorating conditions, and repeated relocation, and land in an apartment in Oakwood Shores, the new, attractive development that replaced Wells. She and her

Photo 1.1 One of the last buildings in Cabrini-Green, construction of new mixed-income development in foreground. Source: Photo by Kyle Higgins.

family moved into their new home in 2006 and have been living there ever since. Her children are now adults; her youngest daughter has a child of her own and continues to push to finish college and launch a career.

Michelle's family moved into Wells when she was five years old, and she never left—a common scenario for the residents living in CHA's housing when the Plan for Transformation began in 1999. Wells was part of a large complex comprising approximately 3,000 units in three separate developments. Wells itself had three distinct sections: the row houses were one of the CHA's oldest communities, opened in the 1940s; the Wells homes were a series of three-story apartment buildings; and the Wells extensions were eight-story high-rises constructed in the 1970s. On the same "superblock," cut off from the regular street grid, was the vacant land where the Darrow Homes, four 15-story high-rises, stood until 1996. The CHA demolished Darrow after one of the most horrifying crimes to ever occur in its properties: in 1994, two boys who were only 10 and 11 themselves, threw five-year-old Eric Morse out of a vacant unit on a top floor allegedly because he refused to steal candy for them. Finally, the Madden Homes, a smaller complex built in the 1970s, sat across Cottage Grove Avenue. Although many families had members living in both Wells and Madden Park, the two developments were locked in a longstanding gang rivalry, which meant frequent, violent conflicts.

As of this writing, all three of the original developments are gone and are gradually being replaced with attractive apartment buildings and townhomes. The new community, Oakwood Shores, houses a mix of public housing, low-income, and market-rate tenants and is managed by a private developer. A new health clinic opened across the street in 2013, and there is a lot of other new developments in the community, including two other CHA mixed-income sites. There are still problems with crime and drug trafficking in nearby parks, and the community still lacks a grocery store, but overall, Oakwood Shores is a much more peaceful and comfortable place than the huge public housing complex it replaced.

We first interviewed Michelle in 2001 at the very beginning of the Wells redevelopment. She told us: "I really don't like it here but I don't have no choice." Michelle told us she had lived in the projects since she was five and had attended two of the local schools. She went to college on a track scholarship, and when we met her, she was focusing on getting training so she could return to the workforce.

> I grew up over here that's why I know a lot of peoples, a lot of people respect me and respect my kids too 'cause my kids respect them.

Michelle's feelings about Wells were typical of many of the long-term CHA residents I had gotten to know over the years—she did not like the violence or the drug dealing, she was often afraid for herself and her children, but despite all the problems, it was her home and she was equally fearful about losing it. In 2001, she had been living in the same dilapidated apartment for 14 years; it needed paint and major repairs, conditions that had only deteriorated over time. She was raising four children: three sons, ranging in age from 14 to 18 and a 10-year-old daughter, Tonya. The family had relatives and friends in the development, and Michelle told us that the resident council president was good about getting programs and resources for the community, as well as helping residents get jobs. Still, the chronic violence resulting from the unpredictable and vicious gang war between Wells and Madden meant that Michelle was living in a state of constant anxiety. She spoke of other children who had been shot and of her fears that her own children could be caught in the cross-fire.

I had a girlfriend lost her daughter in a drive-by shooting and she wasn't 12 or 13 years old.

Q: When was this?

A: About three or four years ago. Like my neighbor friend around here, her son got shot. It hurts these kids to know somebody that is killed by gang-related. That's why late at night, I have her (my daughter) with me.

Her daughter, Tonya also talked about the impact of the constant shooting and fighting.

Q: Are there times that you don't feel safe in the neighborhood?

A: Yeah … When they start shootin' and then when all of them start yelling, turn around, I'm going to get my family and stuff.

Wells and Madden had numerous open-air drug markets, and the police were a constant presence; but Michelle said residents still did not feel safe. The police often did not come when residents called; Michelle said she had had trouble reaching them when she had a "domestic violence issue." The family felt safe in Wells only as long as they stayed in their home.

If [the children] go outside, they have to be inside before it gets too dark 'cause who know when they may start shooting.

Michelle said her kids tried to stay out of the fighting, mostly staying inside and playing on the computer. But she said she worried about her boys every day. Although she knew the other families in her building, she said they tended to keep to themselves.

We don't share too much 'cause they wear their welcome out.

When we met her in 2001, Michelle and her fellow residents fully expected that the CHA would be relocating them within the next year, and she hoped to eventually move into Oakwood Shores. However, there were problems with the CHA's original development team, and putting together a new one created lengthy delays.[8] CHA's own struggles in implementing relocation and supportive services compounded the delays, leaving residents uncertain about their relocation options.[9] As the redevelopment slowly moved forward in 2002, the CHA began closing buildings, provided vouchers to help some families to relocate to new apartments, and moved the remaining tenants into buildings where the plumbing and heating still worked.

Michelle and her family were among those who stayed behind as Wells gradually emptied out. When we met with them in 2003 and again in 2005, Michelle and Tonya described a community where things were a little quieter—fewer tenants meant fewer conflicts—but still overrun with drug dealers and gangs and still very dangerous. Tonya was managing to do well in school, but her older brothers were struggling and running into problems with police. In 2005, Michelle increasingly feared for her children's safety:

> Because you got—you got the gangs, then you got them fighting over turf, and you got them, you know, out in the hallways, shooting and doing drugs, don't respect the kids or nothing, and when you be trying to tell them, you know, just because it's my kid, it's your kid, too, you've got a kid, too, here somewhere.

She told us that her youngest son was really struggling. He had gotten caught up in the gang activity and was arrested for selling drugs. And while Tonya was managing to stay focused on school, Michelle worried constantly. When she heard gunshots, Michelle kept Tonya home and would not let her out of her sight. But while she was increasingly unhappy living in Wells, Michelle was also still very apprehensive about relocation. In 2005, she was still unsure about whether she wanted to move to Oakwood Shores and live near many of her former neighbors, or take the risk of moving out of the neighborhood with a voucher.

> I'm glad that we're getting the opportunity to be relocated. And after they rehab this, if we want to come back, we can come back, that's what my—that's what my section 8 is and my paperwork is on, when they rehab over here, I can come back.

Even though she thought Oakwood Shores was nice, she thought it might be better to move somewhere where her daughter would be around "some new faces."

I just want a better environment for [my daughter], for her to get to know more
people and more out of life than just thinking all about hanging in the 'hood.

In 2006, Michelle and Tonya moved to a new apartment in Oakwood
Shores; by then, her sons were adults and did not come with them—or at least
were not officially on the lease. When we interviewed them again in 2009,
Michelle had been working steadily, and both said the best thing about their
new home was no longer being afraid. As Michelle put it:

I don't have the fear, you know, everybody shoots on the streets everywhere,
but over there on King Drive [in Madden/Wells], it was like just sitting on the
porch fearing, going to the park fearing, just couldn't walk to the store but they
done had a shootout early that morning, so now you can't go nowhere because
you scared to go outside. They might start shooting around the time you go out
putting garbage cans in the streets and all that. Over with. It's love, love right
here. I love this crib. Been here three years. It's all good.

Tonya was less enthusiastic than her mother, citing problems with drug
dealers and gangs who hung out in a nearby park. But she said that she generally felt much safer than in Wells and that her mother gave her much more
freedom:

I feel safer now … because of the simple fact you have to think about it. In
Wells, you didn't have the [utility] bills, you didn't have the locked doors, you
had none of that. And no security walking around—it's just you out there. …
But over here, you've got so much. You've got the police, then you have your
neighbors. Your neighbors look like, 'Oh, I think she need help', and then
they're calling the police. So it's a lot.

The new apartment had some disadvantages, most notably a leaking ceiling that had had to be repaired several times and problems with the building
security system. But it was still a vast improvement over the dark and dingy
unit in the building they left behind.

Living in Oakwood Shores meant that both Michelle and Tonya, now 18,
had to be employed or involved in educational or training activities for at
least 30 hours a week and pass an annual drug test. Michelle was working
steadily for the school system, struggling with new expenses like utility bills,
but managing to get by and meet the requirements of living in Oakwood
Shores. Tonya, 18, had graduated from high school and had a job and had
been admitted to a four-year college near St. Louis, but had had to put off
attending because the financial aid fell through. She planned on attending the
following year and seemed to be very much on track for success.

We saw Michelle and Tonya for the last time in 2011, 10 years after we first
interviewed them in Wells. While they were continuing to get by—and in fact

were more successful than most of their peers—their situation did not appear as rosy as it had in 2009. Tonya had had a baby in 2010 and had had to put her ambitions for college and career on hold. As Michelle put it:

> But she was going, you know, she graduated from high school, she was going to college, and then she ended up having a baby. So things happen, you know, you just can't let it keep you down. So, you know, she's still trying to do [herself].

Tonya had a part-time job at the park district and still hoped to become a fashion designer. She prided herself on staying out of the gangs and drugs that had ensnared her brothers:

> No, it's like I try not to involve myself with that, so I'm not going to hang with someone that does that. And if I did have a friend that did that, I would try my best to like help them out to the fullest, and just, I'd tell them like that's not the way to go, so.

But, like her brothers, her son's father had gotten into trouble with drugs and violence. She said he had straightened out and was still involved in his son's life.

Photo 1.2 Oakwood Shores, the mixed-income development on the Wells site where Michelle and Tonya moved. Source: Photo by Megan Gallagher.

Overall, Michelle still thought she was far better off in Oakwood Shores. The safer environment and new building meant she was less anxious and more comfortable. But more than that, she believed that moving into a new apartment and having to take more responsibility for her expenses had changed her in important ways:

> It's much better than what it was, because when I was on King Drive, it was like if I wanted to work, I could. If I didn't, I didn't have to. Because I wasn't paying rent. It was just like living free, and it was just like all I did all day long was hung out. Hung out in the streets and stuff, you know, doing nothing, you know, come home, hang out and playing cards all night, probably drinking some beers and stuff. Come home, go to sleep, wake up, you know, same thing over and over. I was doing same thing over and over. I wasn't achieving nothing.

MATTHEW AND HIS GRANDCHILDREN— GETTING BY IN TRUMBULL PARK

Like Michelle, Matthew and his granddaughter Amara were long-term Wells residents with deep roots in the community. Matthew's goal was to move into Oakwood Shores, so he could stay in the neighborhood where he had been born and raised and where he felt truly at home. But their family life was even more complicated than Michelle's—Matthew was in his late 50s and worked only intermittently at low-wage janitorial and construction jobs. Amara and two of his other grandchildren lived with him because their mother was a drug addict living on the streets. Although they are satisfied with Trumbull Park, the public housing development where they ultimately landed, Amara is struggling much more than Michelle's daughter. Like Tonya, she had a baby right after she graduated from high school, but she has not been motivated to try to return to school or find a job, and her future path seems less clear.

Matthew's family was among the last to leave Wells. When we first interviewed him in 2005, he was living in the same apartment he had lived in for nearly 40 years, caring for 16-year-old Amara, her older sister, and their infant brother. The building was nearly vacant, and Matthew described feeling responsible for keeping the drug dealers out of his building to protect his grandchildren and other residents.

> I keep them out of the building here. I don't have them around the building—at least, I talk to them and tell them, don't be doing drugs in this building. I got kids going to school, people going in and out. I got a senior citizen in this building, so I usually take care at this point. You have to stand up to them ... then you stand up to the ones that's controlling them, not the ones that's out there working for them. You know, you let them know how you feel about it, because if you don't, they'll run over you.

Photo 1.3 Wells Homes. Residents were still living in these buildings. Source: Photo by Megan Gallagher.

Matthew hoped to get a job as a janitor or as part of a construction crew for the new development. He wanted to make sure that his grandchildren were settled and comfortable after they left his long-time home. As an older African-American man, he worried that he was not going to be around much longer.

> I feel like I'm 58 years old, so you know, the average black man don't live until he get to be—he stay here until he's about 70, something like that. I don't drink or smoke, so that might be in my favor, don't get high, so I might live a little longer than that, you know, I'm just making sure they be comfortable, because I feel like their momma is not going to do it, even though she's around, she's not—she's not doing too right for herself and I'm the only one can do right for them.

Amara felt very close to her grandfather and was grateful for his support and care. When we met her in 2005, she said she was doing well in school and was very open about the many challenges in her life. Her mother was a drug addict, still hanging around the Wells community. Her mother had six children besides Amara, the two who were living with Matthew, two more who were living with an aunt and two who had ended up in foster care. Amara's father's situation was even more complicated; he had 18 children by a number of different women. Amara said she saw him often, but their relationship was not good.

Unlike Tonya, Amara had not escaped the gangs and violence around her. She described being a member of a crew, being suspended from school, being involved in fights, and being arrested. Worst of all, Amara had witnessed her father being shot 12 times during a fight in Wells; he survived, but ended up in a wheelchair:

> When he got shot, I was close to him, that's why I think … that's what made him not want to come around me for a long time, because he thought like he almost had me killed, I guess, because I was just leaving him. … I was walking home from him. …The person came up out of nowhere, got to shooting him. Him being who he is, he running toward the person. … I ran behind the tree. I didn't know it was him. My momma grabbed me. Wouldn't nobody tell me what it was, but I'm crying because I'm scared, though.

Amara described herself as a typical teenager who liked school, but preferred shopping for clothes, hanging out with her friends and going to basketball games, pep rallies and all the school events. But her attitude about life reflected the chronic violence all around her; in addition to seeing her father get shot, she had recently lost one of her friends:

> You never know when life going to end, so you might as well have fun while you can.

Her attitude about life in Wells was equally fatalistic:

> Sometimes I wish drugs weren't on the street, because my momma do drugs, but I look at my momma sometimes and be like, you do what you do for a reason, you do what you do because you want to, people sell drugs because they want to make their money. Honestly, people not selling drugs to harm people.

Matthew did manage to qualify for a new apartment in Oakwood Shores when the development opened, but after a year he lost his job and was unable to handle the rent and utility payments. Instead of simply evicting the family, the CHA relocated them to Trumbull Park, one of their smaller traditional public housing developments rehabilitated as part of the Plan for Transformation. When we interviewed them again in 2009, Matthew had custody of three more of his grandchildren and Amara had a baby of her own. But the family was doing relatively well, and both Matthew and Amara felt life in Trumbull Park was better than it had been in Wells. Matthew said:

It's just that I know I'm safe. There's nothing happened to make me safe. It's just the, the way the area is and what it look like and, and you got, you don't have kids and people roaming the street all night long. You don't have kids standing out smoking reefer or up under your window and stuff like that. It's quiet.

He added:

I go to the store and don't worry about anything. Or walk around this neighborhood and don't worry about nothing.

Amara agreed that the new development was much safer:

Even in the little violence that has happened over here, it hasn't been much, and I can honestly say if they have been shooting over here, I've been in my house and I ain't heard it.

But although she liked Trumbull Park, Amara's life had only gotten more complicated and her prospects much less clear than when she was 16. She attended community college for a year, but dropped out when she got pregnant. Her relationship with her parents remained difficult—her mother was still a drug addict living on the streets, and she no longer had any relationship with her father. Her child's father was around, but lived with his own mother.

We visited Matthew and Amara for the last time in 2011. They were still living in their new development, still thought the community was quiet and safe and a good place for raising children.

But the family was dealing with new challenges—Matthew had developed health problems, Amara was neither in school nor working, and her younger brother—just six—was already getting into serious fights with other kids in the development.

Matthew complained about having to manage his diabetes and arthritis while still having to care for his grandchildren. He told us that he worried a lot about his grandchildren and whether they would be able to take care of themselves. He was concerned that Amara seemed content to depend on him and her boyfriend for money instead of finding a job. Matthew loved his adult granddaughters, but hoped they would move out on their own. The two young children—his young grandson and Amara's daughter—fought a lot, which Matthew found stressful. He was frustrated about being the financial support for his family, those who lived with him and those who did not:

I'm the money. That's another thing. I'm the money because I don't spend money. I saves money. That was my whole thing in life, was save money because I wasn't born with no silver spoon. And I try not to spend as much money as I receive or whatever. I try to save it. And that's another thing. They knows that I got a few dollars and they, Granddaddy, let me have this. I need, can I borrow this? A lot of times I be mad, but I wind up giving it to them. But you don't get back what you give them. You know, they piece it back to you. They can't give it back to you when you, like you gave it to them.

Still, Matthew, now 64 years old, was proud of how he had raised his grandchildren and to help them "do right in life," referring to it as his "calling." And Amara said she planned to go back to school when her son was old enough for Head Start. So, while the family was not exactly thriving, they were comfortably settled in their new community, satisfied with their situation, and getting by.

ANNETTE AND HER CHILDREN—UNSTABLE AND UNMOORED IN THE PRIVATE MARKET

Like Michelle and Matthew, Annette grew up in Wells, first living with her grandmother and then moving into her own apartment when she turned 18. Annette was a troubled child, frequently getting into fights and being arrested. She spoke of the many traumas she faced, including a mother who was an alcoholic and emotionally and physically abusive and her best friend's death. Annette dropped out of school at 16, had her first baby at 18 and has been either unable or unmotivated to get her GED or finish any training programs. As she put it:

> I mean, I ain't regret none of the things that I ever did but, I ain't regret having my kids (well) kind of, in a way, 'cause I wish I could've just stayed in school but when I had my first baby, I just dropped out.

Annette's adult life has been equally difficult. A conflict with another woman in Wells resulted in her being shot four times, and her son's good friend was murdered shortly before we met her in 2009. In 2009, she was 30 and was struggling to care for her three children, as well as two other girls she had taken in. She told us that she felt overwhelmed and that she was often depressed and even suicidal, though she refused to get help. She said she drank and smoked marijuana frequently, she described screaming at her children when she got angry, and she frequently thought about taking revenge on the woman who shot her. Her boyfriend, the father of her three children, was a drug dealer and abusive; she said she was trying to separate from him.

Annette's son, Robert, was 12 when we met him, and equally troubled. He told us that he had behavior problems in school and feared being hurt or killed in his neighborhood. Although Robert said he was happy to leave Wells, he felt isolated and vulnerable in the new neighborhood, far removed from familiar social networks and friends:

> I can't really go outside, have fun 'cause sometimes, I got to stay in the house and every, over there [in Wells], I used to go outside. And over here, I can't even go out the door. I don't even know some people over here. And I don't know if they can try to kill me or anything. I could turn my back and anything can happen. So I just try to stay in the house and be away from everything.

Annette had trouble making the transition from CHA housing to using a voucher to rent apartments in the private market and had already moved twice when we met her. In 2009, she and her five kids were living in a small house in the Englewood community. She had just lost her job because of a conflict with her supervisor and was behind on her utility payments. Because she did not have official custody of the two girls she had taken in, they were not on her lease and so she did not qualify for a larger apartment. She said her current apartment had serious maintenance problems, such as mildew and a basement that flooded regularly. And even though the CHA's service providers had made sure she had enough beds and other essentials when she moved, when we met her, she had almost nothing left—just a card table, a few folding chairs and a bare mattress.

When we met them again in 2011, the family's situation was even worse. They were still living in Englewood, but had moved out of their row house into an apartment in a three-flat. Annette said she liked her current place but said she did not really associate with her neighbors:

> They treat me with respect. Every time I walk down the street, they always speaking to me like, girl, smile, because I'll never be smiling. I always have my head down, and I'll just be walking because I don't want people, nobody say nothing to me. I'll be always be keeping it moving. They like, girl, put your head up and smile. I be like, oh, shut up. Keep moving, and they treat me with respect.

Annette said she had not been able to find a steady job; she said she did not even have enough money to take the bus to go apply for jobs. The family got food stamps through the Supplemental Nutrition Assistance Program (SNAP) but often went hungry when the funds ran out before the end of the month. They got some help to pay utility bills, but that also was not enough to let them make ends meet. Annette said she was so desperate that she sometimes resorted to transitional sex to get money to support her family:

> Stuff that I regret sometime. I mean, we have to make it manage because my kids, we need stuff to go back to school, and I don't be having it, so I will have sex somewhere just to get my kids what they need sometime.

Annette said she did not feel like she could talk to anyone because they would gossip about her or use the information against her. She often felt depressed and stressed and continued to drink and smoke weed in order to cope.

Her son Robert, now 15, had joined a gang and was rarely home. Annette heard that a boy had been shot on the block at 2 a.m.; she worried all night that it was Robert, who had taken to disappearing for days and lying about where he had been.

> But when the boys fight, you know, they run and get guns or whatever. So I'm more concerned and worried about him than I am her [her daughter] because I feel she okay. She don't go too many places. But him, he be all over everywhere. And then the little stuff I be hearing about him being in a gang, then it's just too much. And it be driving me crazy sometime. Like now, he done … and I don't even know where he at.

We were not able to interview Robert in 2011, but did interview one of Annette's "adopted" daughters, one of the girls she had taken in three years earlier. Denise was now 15 and thought Englewood was better than Wells:

> You couldn't even walk up to your house without seeing somebody doing drugs or stuff like that, influencing kids to do stuff like that. And around here, you could, you don't see many people out here doing drugs and shooting dice and selling weed and stuff like that, you know. You don't see people like that. And you could able to walk into your house and be safe and stuff without you seeing people doing dope and stuff like that.

But the reality was that the new neighborhood was still very dangerous; when the family first moved in, Denise got into a fight at school and was cut across her face. She said that she had to fight kids in the neighborhood and at school to "prove herself" and that the family was treated with "respect" only because both she and Robert were part of the gang that dominated the neighborhood.

Denise already appeared to be on the same kind of downward trajectory as Annette. Abandoned by her mother before Annette took her in, she said she had attended 15 different schools. She left some because she moved and others because she was kicked out. Both she and Robert had been arrested and had spent time in jail; her younger sister had run away. Denise stole clothes and shoes because Annette could not afford to buy them for her. She used to get help from a school counselor, but said she had not seen her in a long time:

> I used to always talk to her about everything. She used to buy me stuff like make me lose like stress and stuff like that made me think positive things and stuff. And I won't talk to people when I get angry.

In 2011, Denise had graduated from eighth grade and said she wanted to do better in school so she could get a good job and go to college. But she also told us that she had serious mental health problems that threatened to undermine her: attention deficit hyperactivity disorder; suicidal thoughts; self-harm behavior; and anger management issues.

Annette sometimes wished she could move back to public housing, where she did not have so many bills. But for now, she had decided that she would rather keep her voucher:

> But me going back to the projects, my kids getting older. I'm trying to show them things you can experience in life, the better things for us. We got to do this, you got to do that, you ain't got to do that. You could go to school and get your mission accomplished. You'll be more better that way than you got to hang out and sell drugs and carry guns and all that. It's too much.

She summed up her life this way:

> It's like, I'm struggling too hard. It's like, some, I try to make this right, something go wrong. It just don't never go right. But then when I think I'm doing good, something else going bad.

TRANSFORMING LIVES?

The stories of these three CHA families highlight themes that I will return to in the book as I tell the larger story how the agency's Plan for Transformation affected residents' lives. Michelle and Matthew illustrate two of the more positive pathways CHA families took as their lives were disrupted to make way for the CHA's transformation. Both of them are living in better-quality housing in safer neighborhoods where they feel less fearful and anxious. Both believe that their new communities are better places to raise their grandchildren. But both have had many ups and downs, and both families are still extremely poor.

In many ways, Michelle and her daughter represent the best-case scenario: they moved directly into a new unit in Oakwood Shores. They are generally happy and feel much safer, and Michelle has had steady, if low-wage, work and believes that moving has made her take on a greater sense of responsibility. Although her daughter Tonya got pregnant before she could finish college, she has continued to work—also in low-wage jobs—and move forward with her education. And, perhaps most importantly, Tonya's son will be raised in a safe community and, if Oakwood Shores succeeds, will never know what it is like to live in a community mired in chronic violence and disadvantage. But even in this most hopeful scenario, it is clear that new housing and new neighbors are not enough to move this family out of poverty—they still need help getting the kind of training and support that will help them get better jobs, build assets, and choose schools and programs that will help Tonya's son achieve academic success.

Matthew's family's path was not as smooth, but their new CHA community is quiet, their row house is in good condition, and they feel comfortable and safe. They remain extremely poor with little to no prospect of improving their situation—and many challenges that have the potential to undermine their stability. The family's well-being hinges on the ability of their increasingly frail grandfather to manage the household, and the granddaughter has experienced so much trauma that without effective help, she is at risk for serious mental and physical health problems of her own. Her grandfather has managed to buffer much of the stress for her and her siblings, but it is clear the family needs support in order to address the clear challenges ahead.

Finally, Annette's story illustrates the extremely tough trajectory of CHA's most vulnerable families, families that I call the "hard to house."[10] These families are deeply troubled, with heads of households who have serious mental and physical health problems, are disconnected from the labor market and have histories of trauma and abuse. They were unable to meet the criteria for the new mixed-income developments where they would be expected to work and follow a host of new rules. Like Matthew, many ended up in CHA's rehabilitated public housing, but a substantial proportion of these families moved out of public housing, sometimes in order to get away from the rules and requirements that the CHA was beginning to put in place even in its traditional developments. But moving away from CHA properties also meant moving away from the supportive services the agency had begun to offer its public housing residents and, further, meant dealing with private-market landlords and apartments that varied widely in quality. Families like Annette's that had suffered the most damage from the years of living in CHA's urban war zones struggled and their problems require much more creative and intensive solutions.

THIS BOOK

This book tells the story of what happened to families like Michelle's, Matthew's, and Annette's as they experienced the upheaval of relocation and redevelopment. I begin by using my vantage point as a long-term observer of the CHA to tell the story of what lead to the decision that its housing needed to be transformed, how the process unfolded, and how it set the stage for transforming the housing authority itself. As I describe in this book, the Plan for Transformation not only changed housing and neighborhoods but also fundamentally changed the CHA. And, as I describe in Chapter 3, most importantly, CHA families have fared surprisingly well overall, with most living in better housing in safer neighborhoods. Still, as I describe in Chapter 4, many continue to struggle with poor physical and mental health, weak labor market ties, and their own complex lives. Further, as I discuss in Chapter 5, there are worrying signs that the transformation and relocation were particularly difficult for adolescents and that too many like Amara, Robert and Denise are floundering.

The stories I tell in this book offer important lessons not only for Chicago, but for the many other American cities still grappling with the legacy of racial segregation and failed federal housing policies. Chicago may have had the worst public housing, but the problems of deeply poor families trapped in chronically disadvantaged, high-crime urban neighborhoods continue to challenge local governments, federal policymakers, advocates, and scholars. While there is wide debate about the causes and consequences of growing inequality, even our best thinkers have not been able to offer any truly effective solutions. The CHA's experience highlights both the potential and limitations of using a housing-only solution to address these complex problems and the need for a meaningful investment in the kinds of wrap-around supports that can help stabilize families and communities and help children to achieve their full potential. As I wrote nearly 20 years ago, there are no simple solutions and none that are inexpensive, but without a large and sustained investment effort on the part of the federal government in concert with local partners, we risk trapping yet another generation of children in deep poverty.

NOTES

1. Chicago Housing Authority: Plan for Transformation, 2000.

2. Chicago Housing Authority: Plan for Transformation, 2000; interview with former Mayor Richard M. Daley, June 10, 2013; interview with Julia Stash, President, MacArthur Foundation, March 20, 2013.

3. D. Bradford Hunt. 2010. *Blueprint for Disaster: The Unraveling of Chicago Public Housing*. Chicago: University of Chicago Press; Lawrence Vale. 2013. *Purging the Poorest: Public Housing and the Design Politics of Twice-Cleared Communities*. Chicago: University of Chicago Press; Edward G. Goetz. 2013. *New Deal Ruins: Race, Economic Justice, and Public Housing Policy*. Ithaca, NY: Cornell University Press; Robert J. Chaskin and Mark L. Joseph. 2015. *Integrating the Inner-City: The Promise and Perils of Mixed-Income Public Housing Transformation*. Chicago: University of Chicago Press.

4. Susan J. Popkin, Victoria E. Gwiasda, Dennis P. Rosenbaum, Lynn M. Olson, and F. Larry Buron. 2000. *The Hidden War: Crime and the Tragedy of Public Housing in Chicago*. New Brunswick, NJ: Rutgers University Press.

5. See Susan J. Popkin, Bruce Katz, Mary K. Cunningham, Karen D. Brown, Jeremy Gustafson, and Margery Austin Turner. 2004. *A Decade of HOPE VI: Research Findings and Policy Challenges.* Washington, DC: The Urban Institute. http://www.urban.org/research/publication/decade-hope-vi. Also see the Chicago Housing Authority Moving to Work Plan 2000 (also called the Plan for Transformation), January 6, 2000.

6. The Housing Choice (Section 8) Voucher program provides vouchers that permit low-income recipients to rent units from private-market landlords. Tenants receive the same subsidy as if they were in public housing, paying 30 percent of their income for rent while the housing authority pays the rest. Units must pass housing authority inspection, and the housing authority must approve the rent and lease. For more information, see Margery A. Turner and G. Thomas Kingsley. 2008. *Federal Programs for Addressing Low-Income Housing Needs.* Washington, DC: The Urban Institute. http://www.urban.org/research/publication/federal-programs-addressing-low-income-housing-needs

7. Gina Adams and Lisa Dubay. 2014. *Exploring Instability and Children's Well-Being: Insights from a Dialogue among Practitioners, Policymakers, and Researchers.* Washington, DC: The Urban Institute. http://www.urban.org/publications/413185.html

8. Diane K. Levy and Megan Gallagher. 2006. *HOPE VI and Neighborhood Revitalization.* A Report to the MacArthur Foundation. Washington, DC: The Urban Institute. http://www.urban.org/research/publication/hope-vi-and-neighborhood-revitalization; Robert J. Chaskin and Mark L. Joseph (cited in note 3).

9. Susan J. Popkin. 2006. "No Simple Solutions: Housing CHA's Most Vulnerable Families." *Journal of Law and Social Policy* 1(1): 148–166. http://www.law.northwestern.edu/journals/njlsp/v1/n1/index.html and Susan J. Popkin. 2010. "A Glass Half-Empty: Public Housing Families in Transition." *Housing Policy Debate* 20(1): 42–62.

10. Susan J. Popkin, Mary K. Cunningham, and Martha Burt. 2005. "Public Housing Transformation and the Hard to House." *Housing Policy Debate* 16 (1): 1–24.

Chapter Two

Transforming the CHA

When Mayor Richard M. Daley announced the CHA's Plan for Transformation in 1999, residents had endured decades of increasingly intolerable conditions in deteriorating buildings dominated by violent gangs and drug dealers. The overwhelming violence and disorder had left many of them traumatized and sick. Sondra, a CHA resident leader from the Ickes Homes who I interviewed in 1998 about the effects of CHA's efforts to fight crime and improve conditions, spoke poignantly of watching her community go from bad to worse:

> Only change I see is everything has doubled, gotten worse … You know, it's not a place you want to live anymore … The gangbanging took over the neighborhood.

She went on to say that overwhelming stress had driven her to smoking two packs of cigarettes a day and that she was on medication for high blood pressure and anxiety.

> If you're not a drug addict, you're going to end up on something because you got to have something, and sometimes you have to really, really not see … You got to turn and … look the other way … it's rough.[1]

But even though the conditions in their buildings were intolerable, many residents were still angry and scared when the City announced the Plan for Transformation. Bad as in the situation in CHA's high-rises was, it was still their home. Like Sondra, many residents had lived in their buildings for decades and knew no one outside of public housing. Adding to the anxiety, rumors abounded that they were going to be displaced so wealthier white people could move in.[2]

Residents were right to be anxious. The CHA, barely out of HUD receivership, was going to have to take on the logistical and managerial demands of implementing an enormously ambitious redevelopment plan. And, given its

21

decade-long track record of failing to maintain its developments and provide basic services—or even collect rents—it was not at all clear that the agency was up to the challenge or that anyone could guarantee that the residents would end up better off than they were before.

In 1999, the CHA had few good precedents to follow—throughout the 1990s, housing authorities across the country were wrestling with the complex demands of redeveloping their most distressed properties with grants from the federal HOPE VI[3] program. Too often, resident relocation and community supportive services—a HOPE VI requirement—were an afterthought and poorly planned and implemented.[4] The CHA's troubled history compounded its challenges—its resident population was deeply poor and many would need services and supports during and after relocation—assistance that CHA was ill-equipped to provide. In 1999, the CHA had already received five HOPE VI grants, but most of those efforts had been stalled—some for years—because of litigation or other problems. Only the redevelopment of the Henry Horner Homes, the result of a lawsuit filed against the CHA, was moving forward, but even there, there was significant controversy over relocation and the pace of redevelopment.[5] So when Mayor Daley announced his Plan, the odds of success seemed low and the risks for CHA families seemed extremely high. I was just one of many observers who worried publicly—including in an op-ed in the *Chicago Tribune* in 1999—that the Plan for Transformation had the potential to be just one more blow for the families who had endured years of miserable conditions and broken promises.[6]

BEFORE THE PLAN

There have been numerous articles and reports that critique various aspects of the Plan for Transformation, including some that I've written.[7] Prominent academics have written books questioning the choice to replace the CHA's public housing with mixed-income developments and criticizing the loss of affordable housing for Chicago's poorest families.[8] But no one has looked at the story of the Plan for Transformation through the lens of how this ambitious and risky social experiment affected the people it was ultimately intended to help—the families that had suffered through the CHA's worst days and now faced with losing the only home many of them had known.

When the Plan launched in 1999, I had already been deeply engaged with the story of the CHA and the struggles to improve the lives of its residents more than a decade. Over the past 15 years, I have been able to continue this work, adding rigorous evidence to the highly charged debate over the "true" effects of the CHA's transformation.

My involvement with the CHA and its residents started nearly 30 years ago, long before there was any thought of tearing down the high-rises or replacing them with something better. I first set foot in a CHA high-rise in 1987, when

Photo 2.1 Exterior walkway, Cabrini-Green, typical of CHA high-rises. Source: Photo by Kyle Higgins.

I was a white, middle-class 25-year-old graduate student working on my dissertation, which involved interviewing welfare recipients about Reagan's proposals for welfare reform.[9] Like many students, I had set out to conduct field interviews in Chicago's poorest communities—and like most, I had no idea what I was getting into. Remember that in the 1980s, Chicago was in the midst of a years-long economic decline and academics and policymakers feared it was going to go the way of Detroit, Cleveland, and other rust belt cities.[10]

I arrived at a high-rise in the Robert Taylor Homes at about 5 p.m. to conduct an interview, accompanied by my friend Karen, a fellow graduate student who was about 20 years older, also white, and even shorter and less intimidating than me. There were several police cars and an ambulance at the base of the building and many people milling around. We waited for the elevator with several children, all of us tearing up from the red dust blowing around because of the gusting wind—there was no grass to hold it down. Karen and I took the reeking, graffiti-splattered elevator up to the 13th floor, excited and scared and wondering what we would find.

We knocked on the door, and the woman we had come to interview hurried us inside, telling us the police cars were there because there had just been a shooting and scolding us for coming upstairs when it was not safe. Though it had cinderblock walls and ugly, dark linoleum floors like all Robert Taylor apartments, her home was pristine. Her sons were busy ironing their clothes and mopping the floor with bleach, and she proudly showed us her living room set, purchased with earnings from her new job. She was working as a mentor for teen mothers in the community, which was why we had had to meet her after her work hours. As we talked, her front door kept blowing open, letting in the dust and howling wind, which seemed to me to capture the daily struggle that even the strongest and most resilient mothers faced trying to keep the chaos of 'the projects' out of their homes.

As I continued collecting interviews for my dissertation over next few months, I frequently found myself in CHA developments. Karen and I were generally treated kindly, with most of the women we interviewed making clear they regarded us as a pair of naive idiots in need of their protection—probably true. We had only one scary moment when we visited the ABLA Homes on Election Day—Harold Washington, Chicago's first African-American mayor, was running for re-election. The race was not expected to be close, and it had not occurred to us that it might make things tense. A group of young men watched us come into the building, followed us onto the elevator, and demanded to know why we were there. In the end, the Harold Washington sticker on my jacket, the fact that we were white, and our 'social worker' look seemed to satisfy them that we were okay—and when the leader of the group saw me a few weeks later interviewing another woman on her stoop in another part of the development, he greeted me like an old friend.

I made one more visit to the high-rises that spring, visiting the Rockwell Gardens development on the west side, one of the CHA's most violent properties. Not realizing it was a CHA address, I went alone and once again found the building surrounded by police cars because of a shooting. The woman I met that day had the kind of sad story that I came to realize was all too common in CHA communities. Like me, she was 26, but while I was working on my Ph.D., she was raising her 13-year-old twin sons, had never worked, and was obese and suffering from diabetes and high blood pressure. While I was just launching my adult life, she was already physically and psychologically middle aged. The overwhelming sense of fear and despair I took away from our interview has stayed with me for nearly 30 years and has motivated me to keep looking for better and, frankly, kinder ways to support our most vulnerable families. Even as a junior scholar, it was clear to me that there was no way welfare reform or a traditional jobs program was going to be enough to help women like her to repair their lives.

The following year, a newly minted Ph.D., I was hired to be the project director for a set of studies of outcomes for families who had participated in Chicago's famous Gautreaux Desegregation Program.[11] The program was part of a landmark settlement in a civil rights case against the CHA and HUD. The case against HUD went to the Supreme Court and essentially stopped the construction of large-scale public housing developments in minority neighborhoods across the nation. The case against the CHA ordered the housing authority to provide units in "non-impacted neighborhoods," created a legal monitor and gave the Gautreaux attorneys—Alex Polikoff and his colleagues—a role in approving any new CHA developments, a role that would continue under the Plan for Transformation.[12] The Gautreaux Program was part of the settlement against HUD and required the agency to provide 7,000 Section 8 certificates (now called Housing Choice Vouchers) that could only be used in communities that were less than 30 percent black. The Gautreaux families were current and former CHA residents or families on the agency's waiting list. The Leadership Council for Metropolitan Open

Communities administered the program and held annual sign up days for interested families. Those who made it through the waiting list had to use their vouchers in an "opportunity area." Although many families volunteered for Gautreaux vouchers every year, only 19 percent of them ultimately succeeded in moving.

In the 1970s and 1980s, Chicago's white neighborhoods were still dangerous places for African-Americans, and most Gautreaux families had to move the suburbs to find safe, affordable housing. Later, the decree was changed to allow others to move to "revitalizing" neighborhoods in the city of Chicago. We interviewed the families, seeking to find out if moving had led to either employment opportunities for parents or better schools for their children. Many scholars, including myself, have written about the generally positive experiences of those who succeeded in moving.[13] But for me, the major takeaway was that although most of the women we interviewed for this study had moved out of CHA housing years earlier, many were still dealing with lingering trauma from the violence they had experienced. They were often very clear that they had made a conscious trade-off—moving to unfamiliar communities and facing the potential of racial hostility and social isolation— in order to find a safer place to raise their children.

If conditions in CHA developments were so bad that the Gautreaux volunteers were still traumatized years after they had moved away, what did that mean for the families that were still living in the high-rises? Conditions were only deteriorating as crime rose across Chicago and the crack epidemic swept through the city's poorest communities. The 1991 publication of Alex Kotlowitz's book, *There Are No Children Here,* with its moving depictions of two brothers growing up in the Henry Horner Homes, drew national attention to the crisis in CHA's housing.[14]

The year Kotlowitz's book was published, I was a new mother, working at Loyola University, still wrapping up the research on Gautreaux, and looking for a tenure track job and new directions. A former colleague unexpectedly provided the opportunity that would set me on that path to becoming more engaged with the CHA—and would set the direction for my career in housing policy research. She sent me a request for proposal from the CHA to evaluate their high-profile crime prevention push, popularly known as "the Sweeps."[15] The Sweeps were the signature policy of Vincent Lane, a reformer whom Mayor Harold Washington appointed both executive director and chairman of the agency in the late 1980s. Lane had a mandate to clean up the agency's management and get control of the crime in the high-rises, a situation that became more urgent with the rise of the crack epidemic and the rapidly escalating gang violence that followed in its wake.

In 1992, a sniper in a Cabrini-Green high-rise shot and killed seven-year-old Dantrell Davis as he was walking to school. The crime was so shocking at the time that it captured the attention of the media and the public. In response, Lane launched what he characterized as an all-out war on crime in CHA housing. The housing authority poured hundreds of millions of dollars into state-of-the-art crime prevention programs, police, security guards, tenant patrols and metal detectors. But spending all of its funds on fighting crime meant the CHA had less for basic maintenance and property management, and conditions in its buildings deteriorated rapidly.

The CHA's efforts took shape in the context of the federal "War on Drugs." Vince Lane's own war on CHA crime was both widely praised as necessary and effective drug control policy and widely criticized as serious violations of residents' basic civil rights. Our initial small research project was supposed to let the CHA know how its programs were working and get residents' opinions about whether it was making any difference. But the controversy around the Sweeps and the national focus on CHA allowed me and my colleagues to turn that small evaluation into a much larger research initiative. After the project started, I started a new job at the University of Illinois at Chicago and worked with my colleagues to win a grant from the National Institute of Justice (NIJ) to build on our research. We designed a project that would

Photo 2.2 Security booth with bullet holes in Cabrini Green. Source: Photo by Kyle Higgins.

evaluate the effects of the Sweeps primarily through the eyes of the residents, using a combination of surveys and interviews with community leaders in three high-rise developments—the Henry Horner Homes, Rockwell Gardens and Harold Ickes Homes. Through this project, I began to develop deeper insight into how the overwhelming gang and disorder was harming CHA's families—and undermining the ability of the housing authority to handle its most basic functions as a landlord and property manager.

A year later, I left Chicago for Washington, DC, and a job at Abt Associates Inc., a policy research firm with a major focus on housing policy. As I settled into my new role, the CHA intensified its aggressive anti-crime efforts, leading the ACLU to file suit. NIJ provided additional funding to continue and expand my research and the study, launching me on what is now a nearly 30-year odyssey of following the CHA—and turning me into regular long-distance commuter.

Three years into our research, HUD's leadership took control of the CHA, citing its myriad management problems. Local advocates agreed that the takeover was justified[16]; in addition to the glaring problems of poor maintenance, drug trafficking and violent crime, the agency was unable to carry out its most basic functions. At the time of the takeover, much of the CHA's housing stock was vacant and the agency wasn't even collecting its rents. As Alex Polikoff, the lawyer who represented the Gautreaux plaintiffs, put it in 2013, "The HUD takeover occurred because the books were unbalanced."[17] Nationally, public housing had become synonymous with failed federal social welfare policy, with Chicago's high-rises the "poster child" for the worst failures. As part of its efforts to reform welfare and show that government assistance could be a force for good, the Clinton administration was focused on reforming HUD—itself a troubled agency[18]—and making radical changes to the public housing program.[19] The federal takeover of CHA and other notoriously troubled agencies like the housing authorities in New Orleans, San Francisco and Washington, DC was meant to signal that it was possible to turn even the worst, most mismanaged public housing into a positive force for cities.

Signaling the importance HUD placed on the CHA turnaround, the agency sent its top leadership to lead the takeover team.[20] Assistant Secretary Joseph Shuldiner became the executive director with a mandate to clean up the books and resolve the management problems that had made the agency so dysfunctional for so long. HUD also invested in our ongoing research, extending the funding for an additional two years and adding other developments to our resident survey so that the agency would be able to assess what they hoped would be the positive impact of their efforts on residents' satisfaction.

The book my collaborators and I published in 2000, *The Hidden War: Crime and the Tragedy of Public Housing in Chicago*, told the story of the CHA's final and ultimately, failing, battles to try to salvage its developments. Through our regular conversations with residents, we became intimately familiar with the problems that residents of CHA's high-rises endured on a daily basis. We talked to families coping with broken elevators that left them having to climb up terrifying stairwells and apartments overrun with cockroaches, mice, and other vermin. I once found myself in a building in the Horner Homes where the incinerator had backed up seven floors—the stench was overwhelming and the mess had apparently been left to fester for days. Residents taught our interviewers to always carry flashlights when they were in the high-rises; the gangs routinely knocked out the light bulbs in the hallways, leaving them pitch black and terrifying. The embattled residents— mostly single mothers with children—were trying to raise their families and live their lives in the midst of an urban war zone. People we interviewed spoke of the toll of living with shootouts, the constant fear that their children would be caught in the cross-fire and the reality that random bullets might come through their windows at any time. Early on in our research, *40 percent* of the residents we surveyed in one building in the Horner Homes said they had a bullet come through their window in the past six months. Residents told us about sexual assaults, pervasive domestic violence and drug dealers who terrorized residents and even took over apartments, forcing the women and children who lived there to either put up with their drug dealing or find somewhere else to live.

It took four years for the HUD receivers just to be able to balance the CHA's books and clean up its management. Julie Brown, a lawyer at BPI, the public advocacy group that oversees the Gautreaux litigation, said at the time HUD took over the CHA, the agency could not even produce a list of the addresses of its properties:

> It's just astonishing … We were in court … In the course of this litigation we asked for a list of all the addresses of their projects to compare to original addresses in the complaint to establish nothing has changed. They couldn't give us a list of addresses. They didn't have it.[21]

My personal recollection is that for years, I was actually one of the only people who could produce the list of addresses of all of CHA's properties, somehow having acquired it along the way as we conducted our resident surveys. And I also recall that when Shuldiner contracted out the management of the CHA's Housing Choice Voucher (Section 8) program to a private corporation, Quadel Inc., the situation was even messier. According to my contacts at CHAC, Inc., the new name for the privatized voucher program, participant files were heaped in a basement room, and there were no accurate computerized records. There is no question in my mind that Shuldiner deserves significant credit for managing to take the CHA from complete dysfunction to an agency actually able to carry out its basic functions like collecting rent.

Still, while the HUD takeover improved CHA's management, we concluded that, in the end, neither Vincent Lane's war on crime nor HUD receivership improved the lot of the families living in CHA's high-rises. While it sometimes seemed all of these efforts were making a difference, the crime and decay were so severe that even the agency's very costly and aggressive programs had little sustained impact. Gang conflicts and drug trafficking continued to dominate the developments—and residents' lives—and the buildings continued to crumble. The only time we documented a real improvement in conditions was when the HUD receivers moved forward with the redevelopment of the Horner Homes, demolishing high-rises and beginning to replace them with the CHA's first new mixed-income community. We concluded that, although the redevelopment strategy held the risk of being one more blow to the residents who had endured years of deteriorating conditions, there appeared to be no other viable alternative.[22]

HOPE VI—SETTING THE STAGE
FOR TRANSFORMATION

Beyond balancing the books, Shuldiner's most significant achievement as executive director was to finally begin implementing HOPE VI redevelopments in Horner, Cabrini-Green, Robert Taylor, Wells and the ABLA Homes—paving the way for the Plan for Transformation. During the HUD receivership, the CHA demolished 51—mostly vacant—buildings and 6,629 units of housing.

The CHA's transformation was part of the larger national effort to reform public housing. In 1989, Congress had created the National Commission on Severely Distressed Public Housing. The Commission's charge was to propose a national plan that would eradicate "severely distressed" public housing—what were essentially federal slums.[23]

In 1992, Congress authorized the Urban Revitalization Demonstration, later renamed HOPE VI.[24] HOPE VI was enormously ambitious: the new program was supposed to not only replace the unmanageable housing but also address the social and economic needs of the residents and the health of surrounding neighborhoods. Over a 15-year period, HUD awarded nearly $7 billion in grants to revitalize or replace 609 sites in 193 cities. One of the unique features of the HOPE VI program was that it explicitly required that a substantial proportion of funds be earmarked for 'community supportive services' for residents, whether or not they returned to the new development.[25]

But despite the program's lofty goals and planners' good intentions, there were real reasons to worry that HOPE VI would harm public housing residents.[26] In most cities, working families had left public housing, both because of federal policies that gave priority to homeless families and eliminated ceiling rents, and because of the terrible conditions.[27] In Chicago and across the nation, the developments HOPE VI targeted were the housing of last resort for deeply poor, extremely vulnerable families. Years of living with chronic violence and disorder had left many residents suffering from serious physical and mental health conditions and, too often, struggling with substance abuse. It was not clear how many of these families would ever be able to meet the strict qualifications for the planned replacement housing or be able to successfully use a voucher to navigate the private market.

HUD awarded its first round of HOPE VI grants in 1993 to 40 struggling housing authorities. CHA, arguably the most troubled agency on the list, received $50 million for its Cabrini-Green development.[28] It was not at all clear that the CHA or any of the rest of these agencies had the capacity to carry out the complex real estate transactions the new grants required, let alone develop build replacement housing or provide the community supportive services for residents. While at Abt Associates in the mid-1990s, I was part of a team that evaluated the early stages of HOPE VI implementation.[29] The results of this early effort were predictable—given that most of the agencies were badly managed, had failed HUD management reviews, had housing in terrible physical condition, and had serious problems with crime, most struggled to get their redevelopment plans off the ground. Many botched their first attempts at resident relocation, sometimes losing track of residents who should have been entitled to assistance. And most failed utterly to provide the services and supports for residents that were supposed to make HOPE VI different from the redevelopment efforts that preceded it.

Despite these initial troubles, HUD Secretary Henry Cisneros championed HOPE VI as part of his vision for turning around public housing and improving HUD's own reputation. He and Chief of Staff Bruce Katz pushed the program toward a model that favored complete demolition of the distressed properties and replacement with mixed-income communities that would house a mix of subsidized tenants, working poor and market rate households.[30] HOPE VI development and financing deals were enormously complex, requiring that the same housing authorities who had failed as landlords and property managers to now master an entirely new set of skills.[31]

In Chicago and across the nation, advocates warned of potentially dire consequences for public housing residents, especially the reduction in the number of apartments available for very low-income families. Critics labeled HOPE VI another round of urban renewal, arguing that public housing redevelopment was pushing poor minority residents out of gentrifying communities.[32]

But despite the growing controversy, there was remarkably little hard evidence about what was actually happening to the public housing families.

In 1998, I moved from Abt Associates to the Urban Institute, where I was fortunate enough to find colleagues who had connections and influence to help advocate for funding to answer the important questions about HOPE VI.[33] In 1999, with controversy over HOPE VI growing, Congress commissioned the Urban Institute to conduct the first systematic study of how these redevelopments were affecting the lives of public housing families. First, we conducted a retrospective survey of residents who had already been relocated in eight cities. Most reported that they were living in better housing in safer neighborhoods, but relatively few had been able to move into the new housing that replaced their developments. We also learned that many former residents were using vouchers to rent private-market apartments and, while relatively happy, were struggling to pay higher rent and utility costs—themes that would recur in all our subsequent research in Chicago and other cities.[34]

TRANSFORMATION IN CHICAGO

The Plan for Transformation marked a dramatic change in the CHA's status. The agency went from being a local pariah to being at the center of a remarkable civic enterprise. Mayor Richard M. Daley, the son of the legendary Richard J. Daley who had presided over the construction of the high-rises in the first place, played a critical role in this shift.[35] Many observers agree that Daley's commitment was key to the CHA's ability to actually implement the Plan—and in the process, transform itself from an agency that was unable to balance its books to the typical large city bureaucracy it is today. As Alex Polikoff of BPI observed:

> I'll say the first major change [for the CHA] and a change that's of continuing importance, has been the explicit acknowledge of control by city law ... in the years prior there was the fiction that this was an independent municipal government [agency] and mayors were able to and consistently did, take a hands-off attitude. "That wasn't my responsibility, I'm not running that." ... what changed is that in the public mind there was a shift from the uncertainty and ambiguity surrounding the relationship between City Hall and the Housing Authority to the open acknowledgment that this was a city agency run by the Mayor.[36]

Mayor Daley had already demonstrated his willingness to take on major citywide problems, tackling the challenge of the city's deplorable public schools. He said that he blamed federal policy for the decline of the high-rises and saw replacing them as crucial to Chicago's future:

When they built the high-rises they were beautiful, but the federal government said everyone who was working had to move out. Initially, workers lived in these houses, but they were eventually evicted, and the federal government said the poorest of the poor had to live there. … In the 1980s, the federal government ruined public housing. As Mayor, all housing was the same, it became gang infested, drug infested, it became really a separate part of cities. I took on schools, but the next issue was in 1988 and 1999 was housing. One side of the city was radiant and the other side was public housing, and I saw no future there.[37]

The lead-up to the transfer of CHA to City government control was, like most political changes in Chicago, extremely contentious. Federal policy dictated that housing authorities assess the viability of their housing stock to determine if the costs of rehabilitation exceeded the costs of demolition and "vouchering out." Most of CHA's housing—18,000 units—failed the assessment, meaning that any plan for Chicago would require demolition and resident relocation on an unprecedented scale.[38,39] Before approving CHA's plans, HUD also required an assessment of Chicago's rental market to see if there were really enough units to absorb the large number of public housing families who would need replacement housing. We conducted the assessment in partnership with colleagues at the University of Illinois at Chicago. The study got caught up in the politics around the planning for CHA's transformation, and I recall sitting through a series of tense meetings with officials from HUD, CHA, and the City, as well as the Metropolitan Planning Council and resident advocates. In the end, the study found that, at least on paper, Chicago's neighborhoods could offer enough units to house all the residents who might choose vouchers for their replacement housing. But in focus groups we conducted with CHA residents, they raised real concerns about whether they would be able to find those units—and whether landlords would be willing to rent to them.[40]

At the same time, Mayor Daley and his then-Housing Commissioner, Julia Stasch, were engaged in a protracted negotiation with HUD over City control of the CHA. According to Stasch, now president of the MacArthur Foundation, they undertook a "careful review of building operations and rehabilitation viability" and concluded that "[the buildings] were so obsolete that every dollar you put into them could not be recovered in longer term viability … this was concurrent with the era of HOPE VI and 'let's tear down the most troubled public housing'." The Mayor proposed a plan to HUD that would allow CHA financial flexibility and would also guarantee the federal government would provide sufficient funds to support the proposed plan for redevelopment. HUD rebuffed the Mayor's original request for home rule, but as a concession, gave the CHA Moving to Work (MTW)[41] status, which

Photo 2.3 Boarded up Cabrini rowhouse. Source: Photo by Kyle Higgins.

meant it had more autonomy in how it used its funds.[42] Mayor Daley agreed to HUD's terms, setting the stage for the CHA's return to local control in June 1999 and laying the groundwork for the transformation to come.[43]

Even with HUD's approval, the Plan could not move forward without support from CHA's resident leadership. The CHA had a citywide resident organization, the CAC, as well as individual organizations at each development—Local Advisory Councils or LACs. The LAC presidents were the elected representatives from each development and functioned much like Chicago's renowned precinct captains, dispensing jobs, trash cans, and whatever other favors were available.[44] The CAC had its own legal team: Robert

Whitfield, himself a former CHA Executive Director, and Richard Wheelock of the Legal Assistance Foundation. Their legal representatives negotiated a formal agreement with the CHA, the *Relocation Rights Contract*, formally spelling out the CHA's obligations to leaseholders during the transformation process and guaranteeing all lease-compliant tenants a "right to return" to CHA housing. To my knowledge, no other housing authority has such an agreement with their residents; the contract and the protections it put in place for residents remain one of the factors that has made the CHA's experience unique.

As Richard Wheelock of the Legal Assistance Foundation reflected in 2013:

> [T]he biggest accomplishment I've had in my career was working with Bob Whitfield and the CAC and renegotiating the relocation contract. The MTW agreement—CHA was very keen on getting the CAC's approval of the MTW agreement—the only way CHA was going to get approval was if CHA agreed to negotiate a relocation contract that memorialized a right of return ... that road map that was something that CHA had to follow.[45]

The Relocation Rights Contract defined the terms for lease compliance and the steps residents could take to "cure" lease violations and remain eligible to move into replacement housing in the new mixed-income developments. The contract also specified the services CHA was to offer to residents during the transformation, including supportive services, relocation assistance, and mobility counseling.[46]

With the contract in place, the CHA officially launched the Plan in October 1999, laying out an ambitious strategy of "triple transformation" of places, people, and the CHA's own practices.[47] The ultimate goal was to prove that it was possible to transform the CHA's distressed developments into healthy communities that would offer residents an opportunity for a better life. The Plan set clear goals for the physical redevelopment: demolish the "obsolete" high-rises and family housing and renovate or build 25,000 units of housing, including 9,000 units in senior buildings; new units for families in mixed-income developments; and renovated units for families in scattered-site developments and rehabilitated traditional public housing complexes. HUD provided $148 million in 1999 and guaranteed a consistent level of funding over the next 10 years that would ultimately total $1.5 billion. Mayor Daley estimated that the total cost of the Plan, including infrastructure and resident services, exceeded $3.2 billion and required a considerable investment of federal, state, City, and philanthropic dollars.[48]

The Plan also set ambitious social and economic goals, among them, providing CHA residents with opportunity and access to jobs, education, and social services and assuring that the process would be designed to minimize the disruption for CHA families. The final component of the Plan called for transforming the way that the CHA operated, moving toward a model of "asset management" rather than the traditional model of housing authority as real estate manager. Under the new model, the CHA would still own housing but also "provide financial assistance to other private and non-profit development organizations to expand housing opportunities."[49] Many of the agency's functions, especially property management, would be contracted out to private companies, and the CHA would have to oversee real estate development. Robert Whitfield, the CAC attorney, summarized the effects of the Plan on CHA's operations:

> CHA has changed, which is both good and bad, that they have branched into a lot more than just public housing. Which is bad if you are a resident and you want them to focus on their primary mission—providing safe and sanitary housing. ... However, I think it is clear ... this kind of grand scheme is not going to be successful unless you have a lot of supportive services. ... But is correct to say that is the key if you are going to transform not just the neighborhood, but also the people.[50]

As the Plan got underway, Mayor Daley appointed Phillip Jackson, a key member of his school reform team, to replace Joseph Shuldiner as executive director. Jackson's tenure was brief and bumpy; he was forced out after only a year during which there was little progress on the Plan. His successor was Mayor Daley's close ally, Alderman Terry Peterson. Peterson focused intensively on the real estate development and served for six years, longer than any other CHA executive in recent history. During his tenure, most of the large family public housing developments were demolished and, as discussed below, the CHA struggled to establish a relocation and supportive system for its residents that would meet the standards called for in the Relocation Rights Contract.

THE ROLE OF THE MacARTHUR FOUNDATION

The Mayor's commitment was key to transforming Chicago's public housing a true civic enterprise. But the Plan would not have unfolded as it did without the full backing of the Chicago-based MacArthur Foundation. Under the leadership of then-President Jonathan Fanton, the Foundation decided to put its considerable resources and political capital behind the CHA's Plan for Transformation.[51] In early 2001, Julia Stasch moved from the Chicago's Department of Housing to lead the Foundation's efforts. Some advocates complained that her move created too cozy a relationship between the Foundation and the City government. It is certainly true that MacArthur made a number of investments in things that would ordinarily have been the responsibility of local government, including social services and computer systems. However, it is also true that MacArthur also supported the work of some of the CHA's biggest critics, including legal advocates who sued the housing authority to protect residents' rights and researchers—including myself—who documented the CHA's challenges and sometimes outright failures. All told, between 1999 and 2010, the Foundation invested $147 million in to support various aspects of the Plan, including

- Support for the CHA to create a computerized resident tracking system;
- Support for the tax-increment funding for the new mixed-income developments, critical to obtaining financing;
- Technical assistance to the CHA's resident councils to enable them to participate in planning for redevelopment;
- *The Chicago Reporter*, which publishes investigative pieces on social justice issues, and *Residents Journal*, a resident newspaper, both frequently highly critical of the CHA and the Plan;
- Legal advocacy groups, including BPI, which represents the Gautreaux plaintiffs and was actively engaged in overseeing the new developments; the Legal Assistance Fund, which represents the CAC; and the Shriver Center, which represents the Henry Horner Mother's Guild plaintiffs[52];
- A legal monitor appointed as the result of a lawsuit these three legal advocacy organizations jointly filed against the CHA for not meeting its obligations under the Relocation Rights Contract; and
- A large cadre of researchers to study various aspects of implementation, including among others: my team at the Urban Institute; Robert Chaskin and Mark Joseph at the University of Chicago; Sudhir Venkatesh of Columbia University; Danny Boston at Georgia Tech; and Lawrence Vale at MIT.

Fanton's decision to engage with the CHA was enormously risky. Remember that in 1999, the CHA was still a dysfunctional agency with a well-deserved terrible reputation, just emerging from years of HUD receivership. Mayor Daley had yet to demonstrate that he would be able to pull off his ambitious plans. Julia Stasch had designed a strategy that she and the Mayor thought could work, but there were certainly no guarantees that it would. Stasch said that Fanton decided to invest in the Plan for Transformation because he saw the potential for changing the city's landscape at the same time it could profoundly affect the lives of the CHA's residents:

> Sometimes when you're in a room with people who are just focused on the real estate, you forget the people side. And when it's just about the people, you forget

that one of the big goals was to rid many neighborhoods of the incredible blighting effect of these long neglected (neglected may be too soft a word) … buildings that were depressing of value, crime spots, places of despair for people, but also what they did for neighborhoods. It was untenable.[53]

Erika Poethig, who followed Stasch from City government to the MacArthur Foundation concurred, describing Fanton's decision to engage in the transformation effort as "courageous" and essential for the success of the civic effort. According to Poethig, because of its unique position, MacArthur was able to engage with the housing authority, keep the trust of the residents, and "say some tough things to the City and the CHA" when there were problems that required a change in direction.[54]

MacArthur's involvement meant that other local foundations and organizations were willing to invest in the CHA's efforts. MacArthur and the Chicago Community Trust created the Partnership for New Communities[55] explicitly to support the Plan for Transformation. The Partnership consisted of foundation leaders—with MacArthur having the greatest influence—as well as civic and business leaders. The Partnership also oversaw Opportunity Chicago, which focused on supporting training and employment opportunities for CHA residents, most notably, the citywide transitional jobs program. Terry Peterson, the Executive Director who oversaw the major push for demolition and redevelopment, said that both MacArthur's commitment and the creation of the Partnership were key to the success of his efforts to move the Plan forward.[56]

A ROCKY BEGINNING

The Plan for Transformation meant that the CHA was going to have to displace thousands of families to make way for demolition and new development. Under the Relocation Rights Contract, the housing authority had to offer all of them relocation assistance, replacement housing, and the option of returning to the new mixed-income housing that was to replace their homes. Not surprisingly, relocation proved to be probably the most difficult challenge the CHA faced in implementing the Plan. CHA, like most other housing authorities, had little to no experience in providing relocation assistance or case management, and, in Chicago, as in most cities with HOPE VI grants, the pace of redevelopment rather than resident needs or preferences drove relocation schedules.[57]

But CHA faced a set of circumstances that made resident relocation especially hard. First, with 25,000 units to be "transformed" and a corresponding number of households to relocate, the sheer magnitude of the problem was daunting. Second, as the stories in Chapter 1 illustrate, many of CHA's residents were extremely vulnerable. Because of the terrible conditions in CHA's family developments, most tenants who had better options had left long ago, leaving behind a population dominated by extremely vulnerable families. "Hard to house" families like Annette's were struggling with an array of problems that would make relocating them extremely challenging, including substance abuse, criminal records, mental and physical health problems, low levels of literacy, and spotty work histories.[58] Third, while the CHA had a modest Resident Services Department even before the HUD takeover, it mainly had coordinated small-scale, resident-run programs and the agency had little experience in contracting for case management or supportive services.

Finally, the agency's long history of mismanagement and broken promises compounded all of the other obstacles. As we had learned through our work on the rental market study, many residents were extremely suspicious about the "real" motivations behind the transformation, with some viewing it as an attempt to force poor African-Americans into the far-off suburbs while rich whites grabbed the land. The high levels of mistrust and the rampant rumors created a situation where some tenants refused to believe CHA's assurances, others avoided any CHA-sponsored information sessions, and some refused to relocate until literally forced to go because their building was closing.[59]

Not surprisingly, the CHA's early efforts at relocation did not go well. Most families who took relocation vouchers ended up in neighborhoods that were racially and economically segregated; some residents were "lost" before they could receive relocation services, and even more simply failed to move at all, ending up in "temporary" housing in other CHA buildings.[60] Critics alleged that the CHA was breaking up viable communities and may have left some residents homeless. Others pointed to the small number of residents who had passed the screening and returned to the new mixed-income developments as evidence of failure and a general disinterest in serving its former residents.

A MacArthur Foundation-funded project guaranteed my own and thus the Urban Institute's ongoing engagement with the CHA. The Foundation asked us to conduct an assessment of the CHA's first efforts at large-scale relocation. The agency targeted 11 buildings in some of its toughest developments—the Robert Taylor Homes, Henry Horner Homes, and Rockwell Gardens—for closure, throwing more than 900 households into a hastily designed relocation process. Three agencies, one being the venerable Leadership Council for Metropolitan Open Communities, which had overseen the Gautreaux program; one social service agency; and one small for-profit firm, were supposed to handle the task of helping the 900 households use vouchers to find housing in the private market. Our study found that despite their good intentions, these agencies' efforts failed on many levels. The service providers were overwhelmed by the large caseloads and were largely unprepared for clients' extreme level of need. The result was a chaotic situation with some residents never getting connected to service providers, lack of cooperation between the three agencies, and lack of coordination with the voucher program, which had to process paperwork and conduct housing inspections. Just 38 percent of the 190 households managed to move to a private-market unit with their vouchers by the 12-month follow-up; the rest either remained in place or moved to another public housing unit on a temporary basis. The only modest success was that the picture of the minority of residents who succeeded in moving was generally positive, with most reporting living in better-quality housing in safer neighborhoods.[61]

Perhaps naively, we and our funders from MacArthur had underestimated the amount of controversy this study would generate. We had made a joint decision that giving a trusted reporter an exclusive was going to be the best strategy for handling the sensitive results—and clearly, we were wrong. When we released our study in the summer of 2001, the *Chicago Sun-Times* published the results on their front page with a banner headline proclaiming: *CHA Residents Still Stuck in the Projects.*[62] The accompanying article was thoughtful and balanced, but the headline ensured that readers took away the message that I had declared the Plan a failure, earning me the ire of the CHA and its backers at the City and MacArthur.

MacArthur also funded other researchers, whose findings about the problems with the CHA's first attempts at resident relocation echoed our own. With this evidence in hand, lawyers representing CHA's residents filed suit. In an unprecedented move for three advocacy organizations typically at odds about strategy, BPI, the Legal Assistance Fund, and the Shriver Center jointly sued the agency, alleging that residents with vouchers were being resegregated, i.e., forced out of the projects into other poor, African-American neighborhoods. Much of the complaint focused on the inadequacy of relocation and supportive services.[63,64] To settle the case, the CHA had to agree to a court-appointed independent monitor who would oversee relocation and services.[65] With this high level of scrutiny from advocates and researchers, the CHA's relocation and supportive service system evolved to become unusually comprehensive. The CHA laid out a careful plan for notifying residents of their rights and choices at each stage of the process and engaged a number of social service agencies in providing relocation counseling.[66] At the same time, the CHA partnered with the Chicago Department of Human Services to develop a "Service Connector" program to provide case management and service referrals. While the caseloads were initially unacceptably high, pressure from advocates and substantial support from the Partnership allowed CHA to gradually refine and enhance its resident services.

WHAT ABOUT THE RESIDENTS?

For the past 15 years, my work has focused on answering the fundamental question of what Plan for Transformation meant for CHA families. The following chapters draw on our two major studies that followed the trajectory of hundreds of families as they experienced this tremendous disruption in their lives. The first study was the HOPE VI Panel Study, which began in 1999.[67] The study originally included residents from developments in five cities, including 198 families from the CHA's Ida B. Wells and Madden Park Homes. MacArthur also funded us to be the CHA's "local evaluator," assessing the implementation of the redevelopment and impact on the surrounding community.[68]

Between 2001 and 2005, we conducted three rounds of resident surveys and in-depth interviews with a subset of parents and children—those interviews form basis for the stories that appear throughout this book. The evidence from our initial surveys of CHA families suggested that a substantial proportion were so troubled that they might not qualify for any replacement housing.[69] These concerns enabled us to raise additional funds from the

Photo 2.4 Cabrini high-rise with new construction in foreground. Source: Photo by Kyle Higgins.

Ford Foundation to allow us to do a survey of everyone still living in Wells in 2002 to assess how many had lease violations that might lose them their right to return. We also found a stunning number of squatters—294 adults with 94 children—living in the developments' vacant apartments, stairwells, and laundry rooms. Most of these squatters had once been legal tenants. The presence of such a large population of illegal residents compounded the challenges facing the CHA as it moved forward with its Plan.[70]

When we returned to Wells in 2005, more than two-thirds of the residents we were tracking for our survey were still living there. Many had simply been moved from one building to another as the CHA and the developers proceeded with the phases of the redevelopment. But by that point, under the leadership of Terry Peterson, CHA had made real headway on the real estate aspects of the Plan, as well as substantial improvements to its relocation services and its Service Connector system. Feeling that they had overcome the biggest challenges and gained a level of confidence, the CHA administration was becoming more open to hearing our research findings and to thinking creatively about how to handle the needs of its remaining residents. Over a 12-month period, CHA staff negotiated with us and a group that included service providers and advocates and agreed to collaborate on a large-scale research demonstration. The project would test the feasibility and effectiveness of providing intensive case management to the remaining Wells residents—about 200

Photo 2.5 Ida B. Wells extension. Source: Photo by Megan Gallagher.

households—as well as families then living in the Dearborn Homes, many of whom had come from Robert Taylor and other high-rise developments. This collaboration became the *Chicago Family Case Management Demonstration*, a second, large research project, tracking the experiences of approximately 475 residents from Wells and Dearborn over a three-year period. We again conducted surveys and in-depth interviews with a subset parents and youth.[71] Once again, the MacArthur Foundation and other funders, including the Casey and Rockefeller Foundations, stepped in with support for the research, but in a major shift that reflected the sea change at the CHA, the agency itself provided most of the funds for the demonstration services.

In 2010, the CHA celebrated 10 years of the Plan for Transformation. By then, the physical impacts of the CHA's Transformation on the city's landscape were unmistakable. Most striking was the absence of the massive high-rises that dominated the landscape in some of the city's poorest neighborhoods for half a century. The neighborhoods where these developments once stood had also changed. For example, in the Kenwood/Oakwood community near the former sites of the old Ida B. Wells, Lakefront Properties, and Stateway Gardens developments, there were new and rehabilitated buildings advertising high-end condominiums and rentals, refurbished parks, and a new school.[72]

But while the physical changes were easy to see, the impact on the families that lived in CHA's developments—and endured its worst days—has been less visible. As the story I have laid out in this chapter shows, the question of how the Plan for Transformation would affect CHA families has been controversial since the outset and has remained a point of contention. As Julia Stasch told me in 2013, during the first phase, most of the relocation decisions were driven by real estate needs, in particular, the building's demolition schedule. As she said, "The human dimensions were not really acknowledged."[73]

The remainder of this book draws on our long-term research to tell the story of "the human dimensions" of the CHA's transformation. In 2011, the MacArthur Foundation funded us one last time to conduct a 10-year follow-up for the Chicago Panel Study and a third round of surveys of the Demonstration participants along with a final set of in-depth interviews that allowed us to capture the nuances of families' stories of their experiences with the Plan.[74] I found myself delighted and surprised that things had turned out better than I would have ever predicted. Wells had closed in 2010, and all of its residents had finally had to relocate. The Dearborn Homes had been completely gutted and rehabilitated, so all of those families also had to move. Given that the Demonstration had deliberately targeted the most-needy households, there was good reason to expect that they might be struggling and could well have lost their housing assistance. Instead, we found that most families—*especially* those that had moved to rehabilitated CHA housing—had substantially better-quality housing and felt dramatically safer than they had when we first interviewed them. Further, those that had received the intensive case management services had unexpected improvements in their physical and mental health, as well gains in employment.[75] But these families were still extremely vulnerable—underscored by the shockingly high rates of chronic health problems and mortality rates. And of greatest concern, the children who had gone through all of the upheaval seemed to be struggling, some even more than when they lived in public housing.

In 2012, the CHA asked me to address one of the lingering controversies about what had happened to its residents—whether by demolishing its distressed developments and providing thousands of households with vouchers, the CHA had created a crime wave in other communities. The Public Housing Transformation and Crime study, which I discuss at the end of the next chapter, showed that the reality was much more complex. There was no major crime wave, but there was clear evidence that when groups of relocatees moved to the same—poor, minority—community, they did have a modest effect on crime, becoming both victims and perpetrators of assaults and other violent crime. As I discuss in Chapter 5, this story fits what we heard from youth about conflicts in their new communities, about feeling unwelcome, and about having to fight to prove themselves. Finally, the last section of Chapter 5 tells the story of how we had the chance to launch a second research demonstration, Housing Opportunities and Services Together, to try to address especially the seemingly intractable challenges that undermine the life chances of too many of CHA's youth.

In the final chapter of the book, I describe the evolution of the CHA and where its story stands 15 years into the Plan for Transformation. The problems remain daunting, and there are no simple—or inexpensive—solutions. I conclude with a discussion of some promising strategies as well as the policy shifts, both national and local, that threaten to undermine the fragile gains for the CHA and its families.

NOTES

1. Excerpt from Susan J. Popkin, Victoria E. Gwiasda, Lynn M. Olson, Dennis P. Rosenbaum, and Larry Buron. 2000. *The Hidden War: Crime and the Tragedy of Public Housing in Chicago.* New Brunswick, NJ: Rutgers University Press, page 141.

2. Susan J. Popkin and Mary K. Cunningham. 2000. *Searching for Rental Housing with Section 8 in Chicago.* Washington, DC: The Urban Institute. http://www.urban.org/research/publication/searching-rental-housing-section-8-chicago-region.

3. HOPE VI stands for Housing Opportunities for People Everywhere.

4. Popkin et al. 2004. A Decade of HOPE VI; see Chapter 1, note 5.

5. Susan J. Popkin, F. Larry Buron, Diane. K. Levy, and Mary K. Cunningham. 2000. "The Gautreaux Legacy: What Might Mixed-Income and Dispersal Strategies

Mean for the Poorest Public Housing Tenants?" *Housing Policy Debate* 11(4): 911–942; Willam P. Wilen and Rajesh D. Nayak. 2006. "Relocated Public Housing Residents Have Little Hope of Returning: Work Requirements for Mixed-Income Public Housing Developments." In Larry Bennet, Janet L. Smith, and Patricia A. Wright (eds.). *Where Are Poor People to Live? Transforming Public Housing Developments.* Armonk, NY: M.E. Sharpe: 216–238.

6. Susan J. Popkin. "No Simple Solutions for Housing the Poor." *Chicago Tribune* May 30, 1999. http://articles.chicagotribune.com/1999-05-30/news/9905300119_1_landlords-chicago-housing-authority-cha; Susan J. Popkin et al. 2000; see note 1.

7. Susan J. Popkin and Mary K. Cunningham. 2005. "Demolition and Struggle: Public Housing Transformation in Chicago and the Challenges for Residents." In Xavier de Souza Briggs (ed.). *Housing Race and Regionalism: Re-thinking the Geography of Race in America.* Washington, DC: Brookings: 176–196; Susan J. Popkin 2006. "No Simple Solutions: Housing CHA's Most Vulnerable Families." *Journal of Law and Social Policy* 1(1): 148–166. http://www.law.northwestern.edu/journals/njlsp/v1/n1/index.html; Susan J. Popkin. 2010. "A Glass Half-Empty: Public Housing Families in Transition." *Housing Policy Debate* 20(1): 42–62.

8. D. Bradford Hunt. 2010. *Blueprint for Disaster: The Unraveling of Chicago Public Housing.* Chicago: University of Chicago Press; Lawrence Vale. 2013. *Purging the Poorest: Public Housing and the Design Politics of Twice-Cleared Communities.* Chicago: University of Chicago Press; Edward G. Goetz. 2013. *New Deal Ruins: Race, Economic Justice, and Public Housing Policy.* Ithaca: Cornell University Press; Robert J. Chaskin and Mark L. Joseph. 2015. *Integrating the Inner-City: The Promise and Perils of Mixed-Income Public Housing Transformation.* Chicago: University of Chicago Press.

9. Susan J. Popkin. 1991. "Welfare: Views from the Bottom." *Social Problems* 37(1): 64–79

10. For an excellent discussion of Chicago in the 1980s, see William Julius Wilson's classic *The Truly Disadvantaged: The Inner-City, the Underclass, and Public Policy. Second Edition.* Chicago: University of Chicago Press, 2012.

11. Leonard S. Rubinowitz and James D. Rosenbaum. 2000. *Crossing the Class and Color Lines: From Public Housing to White Suburbia.* Chicago: University of Chicago Press; Alexander Polikoff. 2006. *Waiting for Gautreaux: A Story of Segregation, Housing, and the Black Ghetto.* Evanston, IL: Northwestern University Press.

12. The Gautreaux story is too long and complex for me to do it justice here and is best told in Alexander Polikoff's memoir, *Waiting for Gautreaux*; see note 11.

13. Stefanie Deluca, Greg J. Duncan, Micere Keels, and Ruby M. Mendenhall. 2010. "Gautreaux Mothers and Their Children: An Update." *Housing Policy Debate* 20(1): 7–25.

14. Alex Kotlowitz. 1991. *There Are No Children Here: The Story of Two Boys Growing Up in the Other America.* New York: Doubleday.

15. The CHA's crime prevention programs were funded partially from their Public Housing Drug Elimination Grant (PHDEP) funding, which required an external evaluation. PDHEP was funded under the Anti-Drug Abuse Act of 1988 (P.L. 100-690), which authorized HUD to fund drug-control programs in local housing authorities.

16. Interview with Alexander Polikoff, Hoy McConnell, and Julie Brown, BPI, March 13, 2013.

17. Interview with Alexander Polikoff, Hoy McConnell, and Julie Brown BPI, March 13, 2013.

18. During the Reagan administration, HUD Secretary Samuel Pierce and his deputy, Deborah Gore Dean, were caught up in financial scandals over contracting. Ms. Dean was convicted of fraud. Although George H.W. Bush's secretary, Jack Kemp, was well-regarded, he was unable to resolve the management problems plaguing HUD and the local housing authorities it supported.

19. Popkin et al. 2004. A Decade of HOPE VI; see Chapter 1, note 5.

20. For a history of the HUD takeover of the CHA, see Susan J. Popkin, Victoria E. Gwiasda, Lynn M. Olson, Dennis P. Rosenbaum, and Larry Buron. 2000. *The Hidden War: Crime and the Tragedy of Public Housing in Chicago.* New Brunswick, NJ: Rutgers University Press, 19–23.

21. Interview with Julie Brown, Alexander Polikoff, and Hoy McConnell, BPI, March 13, 2013.

22. Susan J. Popkin, Victoria E. Gwiasda, Lynn M. Olson, Dennis P. Rosenbaum, and Larry Buron. 2000. *The Hidden War: Crime and the Tragedy of Public Housing in Chicago.* New Brunswick, NJ: Rutgers University Press.

23. See National Commission on Severely Distressed Public Housing (U.S.). 1993. *The Final Report of the National Commission on Severely Distressed Public Housing: A Report to the Congress and the Secretary of Housing and Urban Development.* Washington, DC: The Commission: For sale by the U.S. G.P.O., Supt. of Docs and Henry G. Cisneros and Lora Engdahl (eds.). 2009. *From Despair to Hope: Hope VI and the New Promise of Public Housing in American Cities.* Washington, DC: The Brookings Institution.

24. HOPE VI stands for Housing Opportunities for People Everywhere. The program was enacted in 1992 under Section 24 of the U.S. Housing Act of 1937, Pub. L. No 74-412 Stat 888.

25. Holin, Mary J., Larry F. Buron, and Michael Baker. 2003. *Interim Assessment of the HOPE VI Program: Case Studies.* Bethesda, MD: Abt Associates.

26. Popkin et al. 2000. Chapter 2, note 5.

27. Popkin et al. 2000. Chapter 2, note 5; Popkin et al. 2004. A Decade of HOPE VI; see Chapter 1, note 5

28. Ironically, Cabrini has been one of the most controversial and slowest moving of the CHA's revitalization sites, and the high-rises there were the last to close.

29. Linda B. Fosburg, Susan J. Popkin, and Gretchen P. Locke. 1996. *Historical and Baseline Assessment of HOPE VI Program: Volume 1: Cross-Site Report.* Washington, DC: U.S. Department of Housing and Urban Development.

30. Katz moved on to the Brookings Institution and became an advocate for HOPE VI and mixed-income models as the solution to revitalizing poor communities. His influence was felt as far as the U.K. and western Europe. He pushed housing that followed the principles of New Urbanism, emphasizing walkability and defensible space. Another innovation was blending funding streams, including Low Income Housing Tax Credits (LITHC), federal Community Development Block Grant (CDBG), and other state and federal funds.

31. HOPE VI spawned an entire industry of technical assistance providers who marketed themselves to the grantees. Abt Associates was one of the companies that jumped into this business, and CHA was one of their biggest clients. Since I was writing a book highly critical of the CHA, this development was a major impetus behind my decision to leave for the Urban Institute in 1998.

32. National Housing Law Project. 2002. *False Hope: A Critical Assessment of the HOPE VI Public Housing Redevelopment Program.* Washington, DC: Center for Community Change; Susan J. Popkin, Diane K. Levy, Laura E. Harris, Jennifer Comey, Mary K. Cunningham, and Larry F. Buron. 2004. "The HOPE VI Program: What About the Residents?" *Housing Policy Debate* 15(2): 385–414.

33. I owe a particular debt of thanks to the late Art Naperstek, who himself advised the National Commission and advocated for HOPE VI as a solution to the problems of public housing, but had the courage to ask the tough questions about potential harm to the people and communities it was intended to help. He advocated with his old friend, Senator Barbara Mikulski, the cosponsor of the HOPE VI legislation, to fund my research on HOPE VI residents.

34. F. Larry Buron, Susan Popkin, Diane Levy, Laura Harris, and Jill Khadduri. 2002. *The HOPE VI Resident Tracking Study: A Snapshot of the Current Living Situation of Original Residents from Eight Sites.* Washington, DC: The Urban Institute. http://www.urban.org/publications/410591.html; Susan J. Popkin, Diane K. Levy, Laura E. Harris, Jennifer Comey, Mary K. Cunningham, and Larry F. Buron. 2004. "The HOPE VI Program: What About the Residents?" *Housing Policy Debate* 15(2): 385–414.

35. Arnold R. Hirsch. 1998. *Making the Second Ghetto.* Chicago: University of Chicago Press.

36. Interview with Alexander Polikoff, March 13, 2013.

37. Interview with former Chicago Mayor Richard M. Daley, June 10, 2013.

38. Chicago Housing Authority: Plan for Transformation, 2000.

39. These viability assessments were required under the 1998 Quality Housing and Work Responsibility Act (QHWRA).

40. Susan J. Popkin and Mary K. Cunningham. 2005. "Demolition and Struggle: Public Housing Transformation in Chicago and the Challenges for Residents." In Xavier de Souza Briggs (ed.). *Housing Race and Regionalism: Rethinking the Geography of Race in America.* Washington, DC: Brookings: 176–196.

41. Moving to Work is a program for public housing authorities that provides them the opportunity to design and test innovative, locally designed strategies that use Federal dollars more efficiently, help residents find employment and become self-sufficient, and increase housing choices for low-income families. For more information, see http://portal.hud.gov/hudportal/HUD?src=/program_offices/public_indian_housing/programs/ph/mtw

42. Interview with Julia Stasch, President, MacArthur Foundation, March 20, 2013.

43. Larry Bennet, Janet L. Smith, and Patricia A. Wright (eds.). *Where Are Poor People to Live? Transforming Public Housing Developments.* Armonk, NY: M.E. Sharpe.

44. For an analysis of the role of CHA's Central Advisory Council and development-level Local Advisory Council, see Sudhir Venkatesh. 2002. *American Project: The Rise and Fall of a Modern Ghetto.* Cambridge, MA: Harvard University Press.

45. Interview with Richard Wheelock, Legal Assistance Foundation, June 6, 2013.

46. Chicago Housing Authority Relocation Rights Contract http://www.thecha.org/relocation/relocation_rights.html

47. See Lawrence Vale. 2013. *Purging the Poorest: Public Housing and the Design Politics of Twice-Cleared Communities.* Chicago: University of Chicago Press.

48. Interview with Richard M. Daley, June 10, 2013.

49. HUD has continued to push the model of housing authority as asset manager rather than property manager—the current Rental Assistance Demonstration (RAD) program reflects this new philosophy. See http://portal.hud.gov/hudportal/HUD?src=/RAD

50. Interview with Robert Whitfield, March 12, 2013.

51. Jonathan Fanton. 2010. "Foreword." *Housing Policy Debate* 20(1): 5–6.

52. For a discussion of the Henry Horner Mothers Guild Suit, see Popkin et al. 2000. *The Hidden War*, Chapter 5, and Willam P. Wilen and Rajesh D. Nayak. 2006. "Relocated Public Housing Residents Have Little Hope of Returning: Work Requirements for Mixed-Income Public Housing Developments." In Larry Bennet, Janet L. Smith, and Patricia A. Wright (eds.). *Where Are Poor People to Live? Transforming Public Housing Developments.* Armonk, NY: M.E. Sharpe: 216–238.

53. Interview with Julia Stasch, March 20, 2013.

54. Poethig moved on to HUD and then to the Urban Institute, where she heads its Policy Advisory Group. Interview with Erika Poethig, June 5, 2013.

55. For information on the Partnership for New Communities, see http://www.cct.org/impact/partnerships-initiatives/strengthening-communities/partnership-for-new-communities

56. Interview with Terry Peterson, Former CHA CEO, June 5, 2013.

57. Popkin et al. 2004. A Decade of HOPE VI; see Chapter 1, note 5; also Buron et al. 2002. Chapter 2, note 34.

58. Susan J. Popkin. 2006. "No Simple Solutions: Housing CHA's Most Vulnerable Families." *Journal of Law and Social Policy* 1(1): 148–166. http://www.law.northwestern.edu/journals/njlsp/v1/n1/index.html

59. See Popkin and Cunningham. 2005. Chapter 2, note 40.

60. See Popkin and Cunningham. 2005. and Sudhir A. Venkatesh, Isil Celimli, Douglas Miller, Alexandra Murphy, and Beauty Turner. 2004. *Chicago Public Housing Transformation: A Research Report.* Center for Urban Research and Policy Working Paper. New York, NY: Columbia University. http://www.columbia.edu/cu/curp/publications2/PH_Transformation_Report.pdf

61. For a full description of the study and methods, see Susan J. Popkin and Mary Cunningham. 2002. *CHA Relocation and Mobility Counseling Assessment Final Report.* Report prepared by the Urban Institute for the John D. and Catherine T. MacArthur Foundation. Washington, DC: The Urban Institute.

62. Kate Grossman. 2001. "CHA Families Still Stuck in the Projects." *Chicago Sun-Times*, July 11, 2001: 1.

63. This cooperation was especially surprising in light of the fact that Alexandar Polikoff of BPI and Bill Wilen of the Shriver Center frequently opposed each other in court over what each viewed as the best interest of the CHA residents. Polikoff, representing the Gautreaux plaintiffs, argued for dispersing CHA families with vouchers

and offering mobility counseling; Wilen wanted to rehab the developments and sustain the existing communities.

64. The case was settled in 2005. See *Wallace v. Chicago Housing Authority* No. 03 C 0491 (N.D. Ill. June 2, 2005).

65. For a full account of the litigation, see Thomas P. Sullivan, *Independent Monitor's Report No. 5 to the Chicago Housing Authority and the Central Advisory Council*. 2003.

66. Susan J. Popkin. 2006. Chapter 2, note 57.

67. Susan J. Popkin, Diane K. Levy, Laura E. Harris, Jennifer Comey, Mary K. Cunningham, and Larry F. Buron. 2002. *HOPE VI Panel Study: Baseline Report*. Washington, DC: The Urban Institute; Susan J. Popkin, Diane K. Levy, and Larry Buron. 2009. "Has HOPE VI Transformed Residents' Lives? New Evidence from the HOPE VI Panel Study." *Housing Studies* 24(4): 477–502.

68. See Chapter 1, note 8: Diane K. Levy and Megan Gallagher. 2006. *HOPE VI and Neighborhood Revitalization*. A Report to the MacArthur Foundation. Washington, DC: The Urban Institute. http://www.urban.org/research/publication/hope-vi-and-neighborhood-revitalization

69. Susan J. Popkin, Mary K. Cunningham, and Martha Burt. 2005. "Public Housing Transformation and the Hard to House." *Housing Policy Debate* 16(1): 1–24.

70. Sudhir Venkatesh's documentary *Dislocation* also portrays the issues around relocation, as well as the problem of what to do about the squatters who have been relying on CHA's housing for shelter. See http://www.dislocationfilm.com/

71. Susan J. Popkin, Brett Theodos, Caterina Roman, and Elizabeth Guernsey. 2008. *The Chicago Family Case Management Demonstration: Developing a New Model for Serving "Hard to House" Public Housing Families*. Washington, DC: The Urban Institute. http://www.urban.org/publications/411708.html; Susan J. Popkin. 2010. "A Glass Half-Empty: Public Housing Families in Transition." *Housing Policy Debate* 20(1): 42–62.

72. Interview with Julia Stasch, March 20, 2013.

73. Susan J. Popkin, Megan Gallagher, Chantal Hailey, Elizabeth Davies, Larry Buron, and Christopher Hayes. 2013. CHA Residents and the Plan for Transformation. Long-Term Outcomes for CHA Residents, Brief No. 2. Washington, DC: The Urban Institute. http://www.urban.org/publications/412761.html

74. Susan J. Popkin, Megan Gallagher, Chantal Hailey, Elizabeth Davies, Larry Buron, and Christopher Hayes. 2013. CHA Residents and the Plan for Transformation. Long-Term Outcomes for CHA Residents, Brief No. 2. Washington, DC: The Urban Institute. http://www.urban.org/publications/412761.html

75. Susan J. Popkin, Brett Theodos, Liza Getsinger, and Joe Parilla. 2010. An Overview of the Chicago Family Case Management Demonstration. Supporting Vulnerable Public Housing Families, Brief No. 1. Washington, DC: The Urban Institute. http://www.urban.org/publications/412254.html; Susan J. Popkin, Diane K. Levy, Larry Buron, Megan Gallagher, and David Price. 2010. The CHA's Plan for Transformation: How Have Residents Fared? CHA Families and the Plan for Transformation, Brief No. 1. Washington, DC: The Urban Institute. http://www.urban.org/publications/412190.html

Chapter Three

Better Housing, Safer Neighborhoods?

For the past 10 years, I have started every article and every testimony I have written about the impact of HOPE VI and the CHA's Plan for Transformation with this story because it so clearly makes the point about what mattered most for families: relocation meant moving to places where they felt safe.[1]

We met Emma and her then-14-year-old granddaughter Carla in Wells in 2001, shortly after the CHA had announced that it plans for redeveloping the property. In 2001, Emma told us that Wells was so dangerous that they were afraid to even venture off of their porch:

> Well about two weeks ago the kids was outside, maybe about 7:00, and good thing that my kids … are actually usually on the porch. They [the gangs] did a drive by. So it's no different between the day and night. There's no difference.

Carla said it was too dangerous for children to play outside:

> I don't really like the neighborhood. There's too many shootings and killings going on. A lot of the little kids are starting to come out and play because it's the summer, and it's really not safe enough, because you never know when they're going to shoot or you know drive by. You never know.

When we interviewed her again in 2005, Emma had chosen to leave CHA housing and accept a Housing Choice (Section 8) voucher as her permanent replacement housing. With her voucher, she was able to rent a small house for her family in a neighborhood of single-family homes on the far south side of Chicago. In her new neighborhood, she felt safe and, as she told me, more "relaxed."

You don't have to worry about shooting. And ain't nobody going to break in your house. You can leave your stuff laying out there in the yard, and it'll be there when you wake up. It's peace and quiet. You can sleep over here. Over there, it made me feel kind of nervous and scary. But over here, you get to feel more relaxed.

Carla, now 18, agreed that feeling safe was the biggest benefit of moving out of public housing:

Up here it's quieter. I can get more peace up here than I would have gotten in the Wells. I can sit out on the porch and just sit there all night, without having to worry about somebody coming up and messing with [me]. You don't have to worry about no shooting—anything like that.

There are many valid criticisms about the way the CHA developed and implemented the Plan for Transformation and about the mixed-income developments that replaced the projects. But, as Emma and Carla's words illustrate, before the Transformation, the CHA's developments were intolerably dangerous, with more gun crime than any other community in Chicago.[2] I would never argue that the Plan was an unqualified success for CHA's families, but able to sleep through the night without fear is a huge and life-changing improvement in quality of life and one that can and should not be discounted.

WHAT HAPPENED TO THE FAMILIES?

The CHA's Plan for Transformation required resident relocation on a vast scale—most of the family developments were demolished and even those that remained were "gut-rehabbed," meaning that virtually all tenants had to move at least once. Many advocates protested this relocation, arguing that CHA families were being displaced to make way for more affluent white residents, that they were going to be resegregated, and that large numbers might end up pushed out of the city at best or homeless at worst. On the other side, a different set of policymakers and housing industry advocates were pushing hard for the planned mixed-income developments, arguing that they would provide the right mix of tenants and modern design to allow CHA to avoid the problems of the past. I am going to leave the debate about whether this strategy will succeed where the old family developments failed to my colleagues who have spent more time studying the mixed-income developments.[3] My research focused on a much more basic question—what actually happened to the families who were living in CHA's developments when the Plan was launched?

As I discussed in Chapter 2, to answer that question, we followed the trajectory of hundreds of families from the CHA's Wells, Madden, and Dearborn

Homes complexes over a 10-year period from 2001 to 2011. We tracked where they moved, surveyed them to learn about their experiences, and conducted in-depth interviews with pairs of parents and children to be able to hear their stories in-depth.[4] The answer to the question of what happened to the families is not simple. On the one hand, it is clear that resident advocates' worst fears were not realized—the vast majority of the families we followed ended up in better housing in safer neighborhoods. Relatively few (about 17 percent) made it to the new mixed-income developments. Instead, about one in three ended up taking vouchers, which meant they were renting apartments in the private market. Another third ended up in the public housing developments that CHA rehabbed as part of the Plan. About 15 percent ended up leaving CHA's housing system altogether, some because their household incomes increased, and, as far as we are able to determine, less than one percent of the *legal tenants* became homeless. As discussed in the previous chapter, the CHA's missteps during the early stages of the Plan made me and most other observers skeptical that the agency was up to the challenges of large-scale relocation. The fact that the vast majority of the CHA's legal tenants ended up reasonably well-off—not lost, not homeless, and not stuck in deteriorating projects—is a major achievement.

On the other hand, relocation was traumatic for most families, and none of the families we followed had a completely positive story. As bad as life in CHA's projects had become by 1999, it was still home for the families who lived there and none of them *chose* to move. Even family like Michelle's, in Chapter 1 who felt they were better off afterwards, had regrets and missed their neighbors. And, as I discuss more in the following chapters, even when the housing was better and families felt safer, it was not a panacea. CHA families were still struggling with a range of complex problems from poor health to criminal records, and teens, like Annette's children, in Chapter 1, continued to get sucked into gang violence that continues to dominate too many of Chicago's low-income neighborhoods.

Further, the limitations of the voucher program itself affected families' experiences. The federal government limits how much local housing agencies can pay for "fair market rents."[5] These rules mean voucher holders have traditionally been limited to choosing from the least expensive housing in the least desirable neighborhoods.[6] Although technically illegal in many cities, including Chicago, discrimination against voucher holders is common, and landlords simply refuse to rent to them. And as I discuss later in this chapter, discrimination against people moving from CHA developments was even more pronounced, further limiting relocatees' choices. Finally, even when families succeeded in finding a place to live, having a voucher meant having to grapple with paying utilities and dealing with the sometimes-unreliable landlords who were willing to accept Section 8.

Not surprisingly, most CHA families ended up finding housing in other poor, African-American communities where they had social connections and could find landlords who were willing to accept their vouchers. Although some of them ended up in high-quality housing, our surveys showed that by 2010, families who had moved to the public housing developments that were rehabilitated as part of the Plan often reported better conditions than those renting from private-market landlords.[7] A few voucher holders ended up in truly terrible situations, but even those who fared relatively well often experienced considerable instability as they bounced from apartment to apartment looking for better housing in the safest place possible. The CHA itself struggled with new demands: a rapidly-growing voucher program; the need to complete its new mixed-income properties; and a continuing high level of public scrutiny.

In this chapter, I present the evidence from our two longitudinal studies of CHA families, drawing on the surveys to show how their experiences with their housing and neighborhoods changed over time. I also introduce four more CHA families whose stories illustrate the different trajectories families followed as they left their long-time homes, from those who saw only the

Photo 3.1 Bedroom in Cabrini-Green—note the lack of drywall, typical of CHA housing pre-transformation. Source: Photo by Kyle Higgins

benefits of leaving to others who experienced real hardship as they navigated the private market. Finally, I end the chapter with a discussion of what happened to the neighborhoods where CHA families moved. The CHA and the relocated families had to battle the public perception—fanned by sensational media accounts—that tearing down the projects had unleashed a crime wave across the city. To counter this common perception, the CHA invited me and my team to look at the actual evidence about how tearing down the projects affected crime across the city and then had to grapple with the surprisingly complex results.

ON THE ONE HAND: BETTER HOUSING

When the Plan began in 1999, the CHA's family developments were horrible places to live, exposing residents to hazards like lead paint, mold, inadequate heat, and infestations of cockroaches, rats, mice, and even feral cats. For the families we followed, moving meant a vast improvement in the quality of their housing. In 2011, more than three-quarters of the residents we followed said their housing was in better condition than where they had lived before relocation.[8] Our survey respondents also reported major improvements in specific housing problems including water leaks, broken toilets, and peeling paint. Figure 3.1 illustrates the dramatic improvements in housing conditions—and quality of life—from when we first surveyed the respondents to 2011—at the baseline, most respondents reported having two or more serious problems with their housing, as compared to 25 percent or less in 2011.[9] Residents who moved to either mixed-income developments or to the CHA's rehabbed public housing reported the best conditions; voucher holders reported more problems. The fact that voucher holders were renting at the low end of the private market meant more risk of poor-quality housing. The CHA was supposed to inspect all units before approving participants' leases, but was struggling to keep up with the rapid growth in the program—it grew by 50 percent (from about 25,000 to about 46,000) over 12 years. Finally, the foreclosure crisis that began in 2008 hit Chicago's low-income communities hard, and landlords were walking away from their properties, leaving tenants in precarious conditions.[10]

Still, as Figure 3.1 shows, for most CHA residents, moving meant much better living conditions. Story of Sharon and her daughter, Jamie, illustrates how much having a decent place to live meant for CHA families. They settled happily into a single-family home in a relatively well-off section of Englewood, the same poor, African-American community on the Southwest side where Annette and her children from Chapter 1 were struggling with overwhelming gang violence. Sharon and Jamie's story is truly one of "better housing and safer neighborhoods"—and a better life for the whole family.

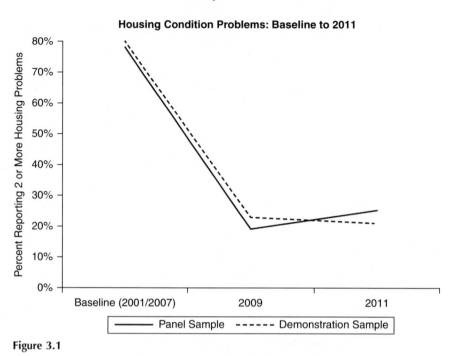

Figure 3.1

SHARON AND JAMIE: "RELOCATION
CAN BE BEAUTIFUL"

I first interviewed Sharon in 2009. Although she was only in her early 40s, it was clear she had had a hard life. Her face was heavily lined, she had almost no teeth, and was so soft-spoken that I had to repeat back everything she said to make sure I had heard it correctly. She had lived in public housing most of her life, first in a high-rise development and then for more than 20 years in Madden Park, the development across from Wells. In 2007, she took a voucher and was lucky enough to find a beautifully restored town house in Englewood for herself and her two youngest children—her older children were already on their own and doing well. Jamie's father sometimes stayed there, too, but like many men in CHA families, he was not officially on the lease. Sharon and Jamie were generally content, feeling that leaving public housing had greatly increased their quality of life overall. Their landlord had restored the house meticulously at the height of the real estate boom, and even though most of the houses around them were dilapidated single-family homes, they both felt safe. Jamie said that their new home was across the street from the "weed house" where the drug dealers lived, but that they were friendly and left her alone. Sharon had a regular job working in the cafeteria

Photo 3.2 Construction at Oakwood Shores. Source: Photo by Megan Gallagher.

of a school that was just a 20-minute walk from the house, and Jamie was happy in her new school. Jamie said that she was involved in after-school activities and had real friends for the first time in her life.

They were still living happily in the same house when we talked to them again in 2011. Jamie had finished high school and was planning to start college in the fall to study criminal justice. Jamie said that leaving the CHA and moving to her current neighborhood gave her the ability to "make it:"

> There was less violence, more opportunity to move around and be safe. ... [In Madden Park] I still was doing whatever I was doing, but I wasn't safe. ... I'd just say moving was a good thing. That was it.

With her youngest child on her way to college, and everyone else living on their own, Sharon wanted to thank the CHA for giving her the voucher and the opportunity to move:

> I really appreciate having Section 8 ... because you can ... pick where you want to live at. And it's so beautiful, they help you pay for it. And you go, you know, you can go in the area that you choose to go in. ... So it's, I think it's really beautiful peoples that they doing this for favors for us ... Relocation can be beautiful.

*Photo 3.3 Graffiti on convenience store door, Cabrini-Green. Source: Photo by
Kyle Higgins.*

AND SAFER NEIGHBORHOODS

The Plan for Transformation was not only supposed to improve residents'
housing, but also improve the neighborhoods they lived in. And here, too,
the evidence shows that the Plan was at least modestly successful: by
2011, all of the residents we followed from both of our studies were living in neighborhoods that were less poor and racially segregated than their

original public housing developments. Poverty rates in Madden, Wells and the Dearborn Homes topped 70 percent, and the residents were nearly all African-American.[11] After relocation, the average poverty rate for the relocated residents' communities was 41 percent, and most were living in the predominantly African-American west and south sides of Chicago.

But it is also true that before they came down, the CHA's family developments were among the poorest and most dangerous places in Chicago, so it would have been almost impossible for anyone who moved to end up worse off. Families moved to neighborhoods that were relatively better off than the CHA's high-rise developments, but it is hard to argue that most moved to *good* neighborhoods—scholars still consider a neighborhood that is 30 percent poor to be in "concentrated poverty," the kind of community that still has serious problems with crime, disorder, and lack of public services.[12] The kinds of low-income African-American communities most CHA residents moved to offered few amenities and services; only a small proportion (18 percent) made it to a place that met CHA's definition for "low poverty" (less than 23.5 percent of families with incomes below the poverty level).

As I described in Chapter 2, the CHA's early failures at relocation meant that the agency had to create a much more robust system and offer interested residents "mobility counseling" to help them find apartments in "opportunity areas," census tracts that where less than 23.4 percent of the residents were poor and there was a low concentration of subsidized housing.[13] Given Chicago's long history of racial segregation, this definition meant moving to neighborhoods that were predominantly white, places where CHA residents feared they would be unwelcome and isolated. The mobility counseling was supposed to help ease those fears and support residents in choosing to move to neighborhoods that offered better schools and less crime—and better life chances for their children.[14] But for most families, leaving public housing at all was already traumatic enough without taking on the added challenge of moving to an unfamiliar and potentially unwelcoming white community, and only seven families from the more than 500 we followed ended up moving to an "opportunity area."[15]

Still, although the changes in official poverty statistics seemed modest to us, there is no question that the families we followed believed they were far better off. Before they moved, nearly everyone we surveyed reported that drug dealing, people hanging out, trash, and graffiti were big problems in their neighborhood. They were much less likely to report these kinds of problems when they first moved and even years later when we surveyed them for the last time in 2011.[16] But as Emma and Carla's story from the beginning of this chapter illustrates, the biggest change was that residents felt safe, many for the first time they could remember. As Figure 3.2 shows, the proportion of residents we surveyed reporting shootings and violence as big neighborhood

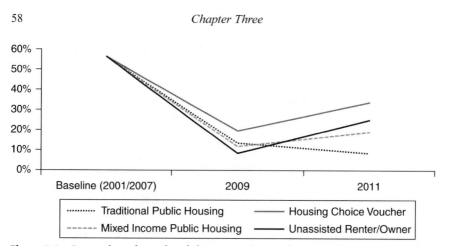

Figure 3.2   Proportion of panel and demonstration study respondents reporting shootings and violence as a big problem, baseline 2011.

problems declined drastically from a high of 69 percent in 2001 and 50 percent in 2007 to 23 percent of residents in 2011. The figure would have been even lower, but, as I discuss below, 2011 voucher holders were running into problems with foreclosures, landlords abandoning their properties, and a resurgent gang war in some communities, and were reporting more problems than families living in CHA's rehabbed public housing developments or mixed-income communities where the CHA provided regular security.

JOYCE AND HER GRANDCHILDREN: MOVING TO OPPORTUNITY

Joyce and her grandchildren, John and Maia, were among the few who actually made an "opportunity move," ending up in an apartment on a quiet, tree-lined street in a community called Rogers Park on the city's far north side. They all agreed that they were better off and certainly safer than they were in Wells, but the move wasn't easy, especially for the two teens. Even in Rogers Park, both faced pressures from gangs, with John feeling he had to fight to defend himself and Maia briefly getting involved in drug dealing. Their grandmother was old and frail and unable to prove much support, and they missed the sense of community they had in Wells. Maia, especially, was very insightful about the trade-offs they'd made and what they had meant for their lives.

In contrast, Rogers Park was the end of a long journey for Joyce, who had moved from Mississippi as a child and then ended up raising her own family in Wells. She liked her new apartment and appreciated the quiet neighborhood. Although leaving her long-time home was difficult, she preferred living in Rogers Park where she felt safe:

> Wells wasn't clean … over there either. … They were selling them drugs and all this stuff over there. … I guess they [the police] waited too late to try to control that neighborhood or something, you know, let things get out of hand. You know, I think cops did it because that was a beautiful place when I moved over there … there wasn't no gangs out there.

When I visited them the first time in 2009, Joyce was in her late 70s, suffering from a number of health problems and worried about her ability to manage two teenagers. She had taken custody of John and Maia when they were very young because their mother was a drug addict and unable to care for them; another younger child ended up in the foster care system. John and Maia's mother died in 2003 before the family moved to Rogers Park. Their father was also a drug addict, permanently disabled and unable to care for them. Joyce was managing to care for the children with the help of her other daughters, all of whom had moved nearby.

In 2009, John was finishing 8th grade. He said that he liked his new neighborhood, but that the transition had not been easy. He told us that when they first moved to Rogers Park, other teens saw him as an outsider and he had to fight constantly to prove himself. He said he was not active in a gang and was involved in both athletics and church activities. But because some of his relatives in Wells were gang-affiliated, local gang members targeted him:

> They used tried to fight me. You know, I ain't no lame [a passive person]. … Because I was the new kid on the block, I guess, and the girls liked me … we would be coming from the church. And like grown people [gang members], they tried tell us we couldn't walk past, and we ignored them. I got into big trouble with the [gang] … because some dude supposed to put a hit out on me or something. … It seems like every summer they do that. … They going to fight me and I'll be beating them up, and I don't play that. … [I have] to show them, like, man you all got the wrong one this time.

Even so, John said he liked Rogers Park better than living in Wells and that he was doing well in school. He planned to graduate from college and go on to either playing basketball or becoming a police officer.

When we came back two years later, little had changed from Joyce's perspective—she still liked the neighborhood and liked having her adult children nearby. Maia, John's sister, was then 18. She was very insightful about how the move had affected her life and about the realities of making such a big transition. She said she had not wanted to leave Wells and move to Rogers Park and that when the family first arrived, the neighbors were not welcoming.

Even though she knew that Wells was more dangerous, she felt less safe in Rogers Park where she couldn't count on anyone to "have her back."

> So sometimes I feel like I want to go back to living to living on the south side because I had the type of community where everybody knew me, you know what I'm saying. ... I would get into it with a lot of people out there and fights and stuff, but at the same time, I know there was like still some type of protection because everybody knew everybody. ... But around here, it's different. If you don't know these people, you ain't nothing. ... So I just try to stay in my distance.

But Maia was enrolled in the applied science program at her high school and was doing well. She thought she was getting a better education than if she had stayed in Wells and told us that when she first moved, she had had to have tutoring in order to catch up to the other students.

> Because I was focused on like leaving my old neighborhood, I didn't want to come up here. I had to put my defense mechanisms on because I don't know nobody around here. ... I never want to let it down because I didn't really know nobody that I could talk to and all this stuff. So I kind of stayed in trouble, but I still made it out of eighth grade.

Maia told us she had gotten involved in selling drugs in her freshman year but had stopped when she realized the opportunities available to her at the better school in Rogers Park. She became involved in the community, participated in after-school activities, and had got involved in a leadership program through the Rotary Club and planned to go to college. As she put it:

> This moving experience was crazy but, I mean, I guess it was worth it. It was.

ON THE OTHER HAND: FAMILIES ENCOUNTERED INSTABILITY AND REAL HARDSHIP

In the days before the Plan, living in places like Wells or the Dearborn Homes meant a lot of bad things—terrible conditions, high crime, few resources. But families could count on having stable housing (CHA was unlikely to close their buildings or evict them), low rent (or no rent, since federal law at the time did not require minimum rents and CHA was barely collecting rent anyway), and no utility payments except an electric bill (and many families didn't pay those either). Moving meant losing that stability and financial cushion, as well as having to undergo credit checks and maybe having to deal with old debts to the electric company. Once out in the private market, families were truly on their own if they wanted to move again, without the support of CHA's relocation counselors or the guaranteed security deposits CHA provided. Voucher holders moved a lot—between our 2009 and 2011 surveys, nearly a third of the families we followed moved, with voucher holders moving more than anyone else.[17] Many reported they were moving to find a safer neighborhood or a unit in better condition, and only a few reported moving due to lease violations or eviction.

Still, some families were facing real material hardship that may have contributed to their housing instability. In a pattern I have seen over and over again in my studies of families moving from public housing, residents struggled with the costs of living in the private market, especially paying heating bills for apartments that were often older and poorly insulated.[18] About 16 percent of the residents we surveyed reported being more than 15 days behind in rent payments, and nearly 40 percent reported being late in paying their utilities. These late payments meant a real risk of eviction or at least of having to make yet another move.

MONIQUE AND HER SONS: "I WAS GIVEN A CHANCE AND I JUST TOOK IT AND RAN."

Monique was lucky in some ways—she was able to increase her work hours and handle the additional expenses that came with living in the private market. But even so, she and her sons were one of the families that ended up moving frequently after they left Wells. Sometimes the apartment was the problem, but more often Monique was seeking a place where her sons would be safe from the pressures to get involved in drugs and gangs.

Like Sharon, when we met her in 2001, Monique was eager to move out of public housing. She had been living in Wells for more than a decade and was ready to go, but was afraid that only people "who knew somebody" were going to get a voucher and the chance to leave. Her sons were then eight and nine years old, and she wanted to move somewhere where there wasn't shooting and she didn't have to regularly run outside to make sure her children were okay. As she said:

> I don't like it too much around here. I think a change of atmosphere would do me better. I really do. I been around here for 10 or 11 years. I think if I get from around here, it's no way I would come back. I don't care how much they rehab, I don't want to come back.

Monique hoped she'd be able to rent a house with a yard where she could raise her children. But her experiences were typical of CHA families that left public housing for the private market: the reality of living outside public housing was harder than she had hoped and she ended up moving frequently in search of a better apartment—or house—in a safe neighborhood.[19] When I visited her in 2009, she had moved three times since leaving Wells. She was happy because she thought she had finally found what she wanted—a small house with a yard and a good landlord on a quiet street. But she was already worried that she might have to move again in order to make sure her sons, now older teens, were safe—her street might have been quiet, but in Englewood, the gang fights and drug trafficking were never far away. Both boys were doing well, involved in sports and had the support of a caring coach at their private school. Her older son was supposed to be on his way to college. And in 2009, Monique said that, overall, she was very glad to be out of public housing:

> I finally had the opportunity and I was given a chance and I just took it and ran. I didn't have to be around them type of people where I moved. And tried to move into a better area. … I just wanted to get away from all the negativity, all the different people, all the no matter if it's three or four o'clock in the morning, somebody up fighting. You hear people busting bottles, babies crying, I mean it was just always some kind of activity going on. And it wasn't always positive activity.

Monique also felt leaving public housing behind had helped her grow as a person and was proud of the fact that she was working steadily and shouldering a larger share of her rent:

> I think I'm a better person because I grew a little more mentally. I'm not around all of that negativity, so I think I grew up a little bit and accept the responsibility. … A lesson that I learned was that even though I have a voucher and they do help me with my rent, but it was a time when I was paying like maybe $75 a month rent. And now I'm paying like $600 plus my light and my gas. So, I think moving has made me a little more responsible and I don't take things for granted like I used to. … To whereas when I was over there and my rent was only $75, I think I was taking a lot of things for granted. You know. So, I mean, as I grew, as I moved, it made me grow mentally. And realized that everything ain't always going to be given to you. I mean when you get things you be blessed for them but you still have to work for things that you want. And I think that's what I learned.

Two years later, Monique's family situation was more difficult. As she had feared, she had to give up her dream of having a house and had moved yet again in her quest for a safer neighborhood for her sons. It was too late for the older son; instead of graduating from high school and going to college, he had gotten sucked into gangs and drug dealing, and Monique had put him out of the house in frustration. Her younger son was still on track to go to college on an athletic scholarship, and Monique was very proud of his accomplishments. Despite the setbacks, Monique's outlook was still positive, and she continued to feel she was better off for having had to leave public housing.

RENTING AT THE LOW END OF THE HOUSING MARKET

Earlier in this chapter, I stressed that CHA residents who opted for Section 8 were, like other voucher holders, generally limited to renting at the low end of the housing market. That meant they were dependent on finding landlords who were willing to accept the rent limits and rules that came with the voucher program and were willing take a risk on renting to a CHA family. By 2011, the kinds of neighborhoods where most voucher holders lived had been affected by myriad economic changes, including the housing market decline, the foreclosure crisis, and landlord disinvestment in places like Englewood that the City had targeted for major neighborhood redevelopment projects. Jade's tragic story, below, illustrates the challenges some families, especially those who were particularly vulnerable, faced as they tried to navigate the private rental market.

When the CHA launched the Plan for Transformation, investors bought properties in poor neighborhoods, expecting to profit from the large influx of new renters. For landlords at the low end of the rental market, Section 8 meant a guarantee of rent payments and full security deposits. Speculators would do a quick and often shoddy job fixing up the units so it would pass inspection—all units had to meet HUD's Housing Quality Standards in order for the CHA to approve the lease. Some, like Sharon's landlord, had done excellent work and maintained their investments; others, like the landlords that Monique and Annette encountered, were less scrupulous. Then either the unit would fail inspection when the lease was up for renewal or the tenants would no longer be able to tolerate the problems, and the family would end up having to search for another new home. The foreclosure crisis added another dimension to this churning, as owners who could not meet their mortgage payments walked away from their properties, leaving their tenants to cope with the fallout. Tenants in foreclosed properties had to move quickly and often lost their security deposits. Because these tenants had chosen vouchers as their *permanent* replacement housing, they were no longer eligible for the more intensive services offered to those still in the relocation process, and the CHA offered only minimal assistance. This situation left families struggling and vulnerable, having to make quick and sometimes less-than-ideal choices in order to keep their families housed.

JADE AND HER CHILDREN: BAD LANDLORDS AND BAD LUCK

Jade and her eight children were among the first to leave Madden Park as the CHA began to close the development in 2003. They needed a five-bedroom unit, and their choices were limited, but with the CHA's relocation agency's assistance, found an acceptable house on the city's far south side. They stayed there for about five years, and would have stayed longer, but were forced out when their landlord lost the building to foreclosure.

When we interviewed Jade in 2009, she told us that the foreclosure had left her family in a dangerous situation—they had no running water and raw sewage coming through the toilet. Unlike when she moved from Madden Park, there was no relocation counselor to call, and she had to find her a new apartment on her own; the only help the CHA could offer was to rush her paperwork so the family could move quickly. The family went to court and were awarded $500 to help with their move, but were unable to find the landlord to reclaim their $2,000 security deposit. To Jade's relief, the family landed in a house in neighborhood on the far south side that she really liked— she said it was safe and had a good school, a park, and summer programs for the five children and one grandchild still living at home. I clearly recall sitting with her listening to her tell me how happy she was with the commu- nity and her "mostly elderly" neighbors. Her daughter Layla, 15 at the time, agreed that the neighborhood was safe, but "boring." Still, she liked her new school, Carver Military Academy, and thought her life was on a better path. In Madden Park, she liked running around and didn't like school; she had even failed 6th grade. But after moving out, she said she had started doing well and paying attention. Her goal was to become a doctor, so she did not have to depend on her mother. As she put it:

It was my reasons. I just wanted to change.

But when we returned in 2011, the family had endured an even worse housing crisis—a tragic fire that had killed one of Jade's daughters and her five-year-old niece. Jade said that her three-year-old grandson had found a lighter and set a bed on fire; the two girls died of smoke inhalation. Media accounts blamed Layla, now 17, for the fire, saying she had been smok- ing in bed. She was devastated and ended up dropping out of school. As Jade put it:

That really hurt her. My baby was in her last year of high school. ... Then she dropped out. She was in the last year of high school and just went backwards.

Jade moved Layla and her other young children to a large apartment com- plex near the site of the old Madden and Wells development. At this point, she was ready to trade her dream of having her own house for the security of a large building with security and decent management. We were not able to speak to Layla in 2011 but did talk to her older sister, Rhonda, who was living on her own and churning through a series of low-wage jobs. At 21, she had just joined the Job Corps and was hoping to turn her life around. Both Rhonda and her mother viewed their experiences since leaving Madden Park as bittersweet—although they did not miss the crime and violence in the projects, they knew that if they had not moved, her sister would not have died in the house fire. As Rhonda put it:

> Well, I don't want to say that, but if we wouldn't have moved, my little sister would still be here. She would still be alive.

And in Madden Park, bad as it was, they had stability and they had community to help them when crisis struck. As Jade concluded:

> One thing I could say about the projects, we all family. ... When I'm laying down and my kids are out there, you watching my babies, keeping them safe, the same way I would do yours. That's what I mean when I say family. We all stuck together in the projects. That's how it was.

WHAT THE PLAN FOR TRANSFORMATION MEANT FOR CHICAGO'S NEIGHBORHOODS

Our research focused on what happened to the CHA's families when they had to leave public housing. But by 2008, I was getting pulled into a larger debate about tearing down all of those dangerous, high-crime developments might be affecting the rest of the city. With little evidence, press accounts, politicians, and community advocates blamed CHA families and voucher holders in general for the decline of other previously middle-class African-American communities like South Shore and Gresham.[20] These accounts reflected a widely held bias against CHA families that because they came from notoriously dangerous places, they must be bad themselves and would bring trouble to anyplace they moved.[21] If the media accounts were to be believed, tearing down the projects was unleashing a crime wave across Chicago.

The issue reached beyond Chicago, with media and advocates making similar claims about other cities. In 2008, a highly controversial *Atlantic Monthly* article claimed that HOPE VI—specifically, giving public housing residents vouchers to use in private rental housing—was to blame for rising crime in Memphis. The article drew a grim picture of rapidly increasing crime in previously safe Memphis communities and then used a simplistic analysis that associated crime incidents with the movement of voucher recipients to make the case that HOPE VI was responsible for these problems.[22] The problem with this analysis was that, as every researcher knows, correlation does not imply causation. As in Chicago, public housing residents in Memphis

Photo 3.4 Sign advertising for sale units in Oakwood Shores. Source: Photo by Megan Gallagher.

were limited to renting in other poor, African-American communities where there was already a lot of crime. They also moved to transitional areas where landlords were happy to have the security of a rent guaranteed by the housing authority. I was one of the scholars that Hanna Rosin, the article's author, interviewed, and so got caught up in the ensuing controversy. Like the majority of the other researchers she cited, I believed—and still believe today—that she twisted the evidence to fit a story line that had little basis in fact. Because of the article, I joined in the national debate about the impact of housing vouchers on crime, arguing that there was no evidence to justify blaming public housing transformation for broader trends.[23]

The issue of how tearing down public housing was affecting "receiving" neighborhoods, i.e., the places where former residents moved, continued to simmer. In 2010, the CHA marked the 10th anniversary of the Plan for Transformation with a conference and celebration, happily touting our findings of generally positive outcomes for CHA families. They surprised me by asking if I would take on the challenge of finding out what effect tearing down the projects really had on crime in Chicago. It was a bold move: the CHA was asking me to publicly take on what had become the most controversial aspect of public housing transformation across the nation. And it was good timing—I had run into Wes Skogan, a former professor of mine from

Northwestern, who studied longitudinal crime trends in Chicago and was eager to take on the question of the impact of the Plan on crime citywide.

At the CHA's request, the MacArthur Foundation provided funding for this new research, and the housing authority provided us with its extensive database on where residents had moved over the 10 years from 1999 to 2010. I engaged my colleague, George Galster, who had studied the impact of vouchers on property values, and we began to map out the complex analysis that answering this question would require.[24]

We were fortunate to also have a set of research partners in Atlanta exploring the same issues who could help us develop the robust research design that would stand up to the inevitable criticism. The Atlanta Housing Authority (AHA) had also undertaken public housing transformation on a large scale, tearing down virtually all of its public housing and replacing it with mixed-income communities and vouchers. Their executive director, Renee Glover, had famously championed her approach as a national model. But by 2010, she was also concerned about the accusations in *The Atlantic* story and was willing to provide data for a similar analysis.[25]

Answering the question of how relocating public housing residents into private-market housing affected crime rates in Chicago and Atlanta required extremely rigorous analysis. Because of the sensitivity of the subject matter and the complexity of the analytic methods, we subjected our work to a thorough review—any interested readers should refer to the journal articles cited in the notes.[26] What we found did not support the popular myth, but it was also a less rosy picture than the two housing authorities would have liked, and the release process involved extensive vetting all around.

Essentially, we found no evidence that tearing down the projects caused a citywide crime wave—quite the contrary—but we also found that there were some negative consequences for the places where former residents moved. In both cities, tearing down public housing brought large and lasting decreases in crime in the places where the developments had stood.[27] These decreases in crime in the former public housing neighborhoods contributed to a small but significant net decrease in violent crime across both cities. In Chicago, the biggest impact was a reduction in overall gun crime, which had been concentrated in CHA's properties.

At the same time, the picture was not entirely positive. The transformation contributed to slightly higher rate of property crime overall in Chicago, and some neighborhoods in both cities experienced problems because of the new residents. The story is complicated because crime was dropping dramatically in both Chicago and Atlanta throughout the 2000s, even in the low-income neighborhoods where relocated residents found housing. These neighborhoods did not experience an actual increase in violent crime, but our analysis showed that once the number of relocated households reached a certain threshold, crime rates, on average, *decreased less than they would have* if no public housing families had moved there.[28] The simplest way to understand this finding is that crime did not go up when CHA or AHA families moved into different neighborhoods, but their arrival kept crime from continuing to go down. That subtle distinction was probably lost on their neighbors; if there was a crime on their block, it was easy to blame the new residents for the problem. And the focus groups we conducted across the city confirmed that residents everywhere, even in areas where there were only a handful of relocated families, believed that tearing down the projects had brought crime and trouble to their neighborhoods.[29]

Despite our research and that of other scholars who replicated our findings about the effects of public housing relocation on crime in other cities, this story of a clear linkage between public housing transformation and rising crime remains remarkably difficult to debunk. An indicator of the mythology surrounding CHA residents is that I continue to get calls from reporters in places as far away from Chicago as Iowa and Indiana pursuing stories that blame former CHA families for homicides in their cities—even in the face of the evidence that almost no CHA households actually moved outside the city limits.[30]

And while the evidence shows that Chicago's public housing transformation did not lead to a wave of violent crime anywhere else in the city, the fact that crime stopped going down in the communities where former residents moved suggests some reason for concern. As I will discuss more in Chapter 5, the complex geography of Chicago's violent gangs meant that, in reality, CHA families were often moving into hostile territory. Teens like Joyce's grandson John, Monique's older son, and Annette's son Robert from Chapter 1 ended up fighting to defend themselves, and sometimes became part of the drug dealing and gang turf battles in their new communities. At the CHA's request, we did a follow-up analysis to the broader crime study to try to see if we could determine whether CHA youth were more likely to be victims or perpetrators of crime and found that it was impossible to tell, suggesting that they were generally being caught up in the local gang conflicts.[31]

A NEED FOR BETTER SERVICES
AND SUPPORT FOR CHA FAMILIES

As the stories in this chapter show, the Plan for Transformation had profound effects—both good and bad—on the lives of CHA families. The Plan enabled—or forced—families to leave the CHA's decaying, high-crime developments. Residents had mixed reactions to being told they were going to have to leave, with some eager to find a better life and others mourning the loss of the communities where they and their families had lived for generations. What they found when they left CHA's housing was in many ways better than what many had feared: most ended up in decent housing in neighborhoods where they and their children felt safe, some for the first time in their lives. But as Monique and Jade's stories show, their experiences weren't always good, and families faced new challenges, including new expenses and unreliable landlords. And as the story of Joyce and her grandchildren John and Maia clearly illustrates, these relocated residents often faced unwelcoming—and sometimes hostile—neighbors.

Taken together, these stories highlight the fact that relocation alone was not enough to address the deep needs of many of CHA's residents. At the time the Plan for Transformation began, the CHA was home to some of the most vulnerable and needy families in the city, many of whom had little or no experience living anywhere else. Further, living in CHA's violent developments meant that most residents were dealing with the effects of chronic trauma, effects that undermined their physical and mental health and their ability to cope with the new challenges of living outside public housing. Even those who were doing well struggled with the unfamiliar challenges of navigating life outside of CHA's developments. Youth, in particular, struggled with living in unfamiliar and sometimes hostile neighborhoods where they lacked the protection of their friends and associates from public housing.

In sum, there is no doubt that the CHA's Plan for Transformation was a successful housing intervention overall—it met its basic goal of providing families with an improved living environment. Given where the CHA started, this success is an enormous achievement. But better housing alone was not enough to address the deep needs of many of CHA's families. In the next chapters, I first talk about the larger barriers that keep CHA families from moving forward and the intensive service approach we developed and tested—in partnership with the CHA. Then I turn to the sad story of CHA's youth and the clear need to find solutions for the next generation.

NOTES

1. This finding is also consistent with what we heard from families in the Moving to Opportunity Demonstration. See Xavier de Souza Briggs, Susan J. Popkin, and John Goering. 2010. *Moving to Opportunity: The Story of an American Experiment to Fight Ghetto Poverty.* Oxford: Oxford University Press.

2. Susan J. Popkin, Michael J. Rich, Leah Hendey, Chris Hayes, Joseph Parilla, and George Galster. 2012. "Public Housing Transformation and Crime: Making the Case for Responsible Relocation." *Cityscape* 14(3): 137–160. http://www.huduser.org/portal/periodicals/cityscpe/vol14num3/Cityscape_Nov2012_pub_house_trans.pdf.

3. See for example Robert J. Chaskin and Mark L. Joseph. 2015. *Integrating the Inner-City: The Promise and Perils of Mixed-Income Public Housing Transformation.* Chicago: University of Chicago Press.

4. The Chicago Panel Study tracked and surveyed a group of 198 former residents of Madden and Wells since 2001; our Chicago Family Case Management Demonstration surveyed the 475 "hard to house" residents of Madden, Wells, and Dearborn who received intensive case management and wrap-around services, including case management, clinical mental health counseling, transitional jobs, financial literacy workshops, substance abuse treatment, and enhanced mobility counseling. In 2011, we combined these samples to assess the long-term outcomes for CHA residents who had to relocate because their original public housing development was slated for demolition or rehabilitation. For details on the studies and research methods, see http://www.urban.org/features/cha-families-and-plan-transformation

5. For information on how HUD sets Fair Market Rents, see https://portal.hud.gov/hudportal/documents/huddoc?id=DOC_8402.pdf

6. The Supreme Court ruling in *Texas Department of Housing v. the Inclusive Communities Project* and the new HUD regulations may finally change the patterns of segregation in the Housing Choice Voucher program. http://www.washingtonpost.com/blogs/wonkblog/wp/2015/07/08/obama-administration-to-unveil-major-new-rules-targeting-segregation-across-u-s/.

7. Susan J. Popkin. 2010. "A Glass Half-Empty: Public Housing Families in Transition." *Housing Policy Debate* 20(1): 42–62.

8. Larry Buron, Christopher Hayes, and Chantal Hailey. 2013. An Improved Living Environment, but … Long-Term Outcomes for CHA Residents, Brief No. 3. Washington, DC: The Urban Institute. http://www.urban.org/research/publication/improved-living-environment.

9. This finding is also consistent with finding from the Moving to Opportunity study. See Jennifer Comey, Susan J. Popkin, and Kaitlin Franks. 2012. "MTO: A Successful Housing Intervention." *Cityscape* 14(2): 87–107.

10. Our in-depth interviews with voucher holders suggest some of this growth may be due to the national foreclosure crisis, which has forced renters to quickly find a new place when the landlord faces foreclosure.

11. The poverty rate in Madden and Wells was 72 percent; the rate was 78 percent in Dearborn. Both communities were almost entirely African-American. The share of residents living in poverty and racial concentration is assessed at the census tract level. Census 2000 is the data source for the original developments. Current Housing data are attained from the American Community Survey five-year 2005–2010 estimates (poverty rate) and Census 2010 (racial concentration).

12. See Robert Sampson's definition of a chronically disadvantaged community, in Robert J. Sampson. 2012. *Great American City: Chicago and the Enduring Neighborhood Effect.* Chicago: University of Chicago Press.

13. The CHA's current definition of opportunity areas can be found here: http://www.thecha.org/residents/services/mobility-counseling-program/.

14. New research on the Moving to Opportunity Demonstration suggests that children who move from public housing to opportunity neighborhoods fare better

economically as adults. See Raj Chetty, Nathaniel Hendren, and Lawrence F. Katz. 2015. The Effects of Exposure to Better Neighborhood Environments on Children: New Evidence from the Moving to Opportunity Experiment. Cambridge: National Bureau of Economic Research. http://www.equality-of-pportunity.org/images/mto_paper.pdf

15. Definition from http://www.thecha.org/pages/opp_map/2662.php

16. See Buron et al. 2013. Chapter 3. note 8. and Popkin. 2010. Chapter 3, note 7.

17. Since the 2009 survey, 43 percent of voucher holders moved once or more and seven percent moved twice or more. About 26 percent of mixed-income residents moved once or more, and only 18 percent in traditional public housing moved once or more, almost all of them only once. Nonassisted respondents had moved at much higher raters: 56 percent moved *once* or more, and eight percent moved multiple times.

18. See Susan J., Popkin, Diane K. Levy, and Larry Buron. 2009. "Has HOPE VI Transformed Residents' Lives? New Evidence from the HOPE VI Panel Study." *Housing Studies* 24(4): 477–502 and Comey et al. Chapter 3, note 9.

19. The CHA families' struggles with vouchers in the private market are similar to those documented in other research, including research on the Moving to Opportunity Demonstration. See Briggs, Popkin, and Goering. 2010. Chapter, 3, note 1.

20. See, for example, Mitch Dumke, "A Neighborhood's Steady Decline," *New York Times*, April 28, 2011, http://www.nytimes.com/2011/04/29/us/29cncguns.html; and Jennifer Medina, "Subsidies and Suspicion," *New York Times*, August 11, 2011, http://www.nytimes.com/2011/08/11/us/11housing.html?_r=2&src=me&ref=us

21. We heard these views—and worse—reflected in focus groups we conducted in 2011 with residents in different communities across the city where CHA families moved. See Popkin, Rich et al. 2012. Chapter 3, note 2; Susan J. Popkin, Michael J. Rich, Leah Hendey, Christopher Hayes, and Joseph Parilla. 2012. *Public Housing Transformation and Crime: Making the Case for Responsible Relocation.* Washington, DC: The Urban Institute. http://www.urban.org/research/publication/public-housing-transformation-and-crime-making-case-responsible-relocation.

22. Hanna Rosin. 2008. "American Murder Mystery." *The Atlantic Monthly* 302(1): 40–54.

23. See Xavier de Souza Briggs and Peter Dreier. 2008. "Memphis Murder Mystery? No, Just Mistaken Identity." *Shelterforce*, Posted July 22, 2008. http://www.shelterforce.org/article/special/1043.

24. George Galster led the design of the complex analysis of relocation and crime trends. Wesley Skogan provided a historical database of crime trends at the census tract level. Leah Hendey and Chris Hayes conducted most of the complex analyses under their guidance, and we had the research vetted by several experts in econometric modeling and criminology. Michael Rich of Emory University led the companion analysis of crime trends in Atlanta. See Popkin, Rich et al. 2012. and Leah Hendey, George C. Galster, Susan J. Popkin, and Chris Hayes. 2015. "Housing Choice Voucher Holders and Neighborhood Crime: A Dynamic Panel Analysis." *Urban Affairs Review.* http://uar.sagepub.com/content/early/2015/06/30/1078087415591348.full.pdf+html.

25. The Annie E. Casey Foundation funded the Atlanta portion of the research.

26. See also Susan J. Popkin, Michael J. Rich, Leah Hendey, Christopher Hayes, and Joseph Parilla. 2012. *Public Housing Transformation and Crime: Making the Case for Responsible Relocation*. Washington, DC: The Urban Institute. http://www. urban.org/research/publication/public-housing-transformation-and-crime-making-case-responsible-relocation and Christopher Hayes, Graham McDonald, Susan Popkin, Leah Hendey, and Allison Stolte. 2013. Public Housing Transformation and Crime: Are Relocatees More Likely to be Offenders or Victims? *Cityscape* 15(3): 9–35.

27. We define neighborhoods as census tracts in this analysis. Throughout this brief, the terms "neighborhood," "census tract," and "tract" are used interchangeably. These are not in reference to Chicago's 77 community areas, which are much larger, typically containing around nine census tracts.

28. Responsible relocation is a strategy that provides relocation counseling and other direct services to ensure that residents receive appropriate relocation benefits and have the opportunity to move to better neighborhoods than those they are leaving.

29. See Popkin, Rich et al. 2012, note 26.

30. The Lafayette Journal and Courier did an excellent investigation of the persistence of the story of link between relocated CHA families and crime: http://www. jconline.com/story/news/2014/10/17/truth-black-white/17293817/.

31. See Christopher Hayes, Graham McDonald, Susan Popkin, Leah Hendey, and Allison Stolte. 2013. "Public Housing Transformation and Crime: Are Relocatees More Likely to be Offenders or Victims?" *Cityscape* 15(3): 9–35.

Chapter Four

The Hard to House

In the last chapter, I told the story of the biggest achievement of the CHA's Plan for Transformation—successfully moving most of the families in the agency's worst developments to better housing in safer neighborhoods. But there is another important story that is key to understanding how the Plan affected residents' lives, namely the recognition that better housing was not enough. The families that had remained in CHA's developments as conditions deteriorated had deeper needs that required more complex solutions. In this chapter, I tell the story of how, after its initial stumbles, the CHA came to partner with me and a team of local social service agencies to develop a set of relocation and supportive services for residents that would substantially improve the trajectory for some of its most vulnerable families. The legacy of what became the Chicago Family Case Management Demonstration is the exceptionally robust resident services department CHA has maintained for nearly a decade, one that, as of this writing, is the envy of housing authorities across the nation.

As I said in Chapter 3, given the CHA's history, there was little reason to expect that the agency would succeed in pulling off the massive relocation and complex real estate transactions the Plan required. The odds of its being able to develop and implement effective relocation and supportive services for its residents seemed even lower. HUD had taken control of the CHA because the agency had failed to manage its properties and its finances. The receivership was primarily aimed at addressing those basic failings and at laying the groundwork for the Plan. HUD itself had little experience in overseeing large-scale resident relocation and supportive services and was just beginning to seriously try to track what HOPE VI grant recipients were doing with their Community Supportive Service (CSS) dollars. And, as I've shown, in 1999 when the Plan launched, CHA's resident population was dominated by extremely needy, highly vulnerable families. These households were grappling with a range of problems, including lease violations, poor credit, bad debt, criminal records, and serious physical and mental health problems, all of which meant that they were going to face steep challenges in qualifying for the new mixed-income housing or even finding a private-market landlord who would accept their vouchers. In a paper we wrote in 2005, we labeled these vulnerable families the "hard to house" to call attention to the fact that they were being left behind as the CHA began to empty out its developments.[1]

THE HARD TO HOUSE—COMPLEX SITUATIONS WITH NO SIMPLE SOLUTIONS

Before moving to the story of how the CHA ultimately came to accept and embrace a new approach to supportive services, I introduce a set of residents whose stories paint a picture of the kinds of daunting challenges that made these families "hard to house." But I think it is first important step back and acknowledge an uncomfortable reality: people could argue—as even some CHA resident leaders did—that some of the "hard to house" were responsible for making life in CHA miserable for everyone else and that they should be evicted/kept out of the new mixed-income housing. This group included the alcoholics, drug addicts, drug dealers, gang bangers, mentally ill, and families whose violent conflicts spilled out of their apartments into the public space. They were, frankly, the kinds of people most of us would prefer to avoid having as neighbors. And there were and are no simple or low-cost solutions to addressing their deep and complex problems. On the other hand, most of the "hard to house" were long-time CHA residents and had endured the worst days of CHA's decline. They had experienced the kind of trauma that leaves permanent physical and psychological scars. Many had experienced physical harm from hazards like lead paint, mold, unprotected radiators, darkened stairwells, and getting caught up in the chronic violence. Finally, there is the other reality that the terrible conditions were the direct result of federal and local policy failures: deliberate racial and economic segregation and neglect. "Hard to house" tenants might be unsympathetic, but not trying to help them would mean not acknowledging this history—and also the cold reality that, without effective help, they and their problems have real economic and social cost for us all.

ANNETTE, CARL, AND ERICA—FAMILIES WITH COMPLEX PROBLEMS

In Chapter 1, I introduced Annette and her five children, a family facing chronic instability and serious troubles. Annette was a lifelong CHA resident, living in Wells when the Plan was announced. She had a long history of trauma, substance abuse, and violent behavior and was struggling to care for her children. Although she worked off and on, her employment history was spotty at best and, when I first met her, she'd just lost a job after getting into a fight with her supervisor. She and her two oldest children were clearly seriously depressed. Both of the teens were gradually being drawn into risky and dangerous behavior, the son becoming increasingly involved in gangs and fighting and the daughter into trading sex for money to pay for basic necessities for herself and the other children in the household. The CHA's basic services could not possibly meet all of Annette's family's complex and long-term needs. Simply keeping this family stable and off the streets would require an intensive, long-term commitment.

Carl and his son Harry from the Dearborn Homes also needed that kind of sustained, intensive support. Carl was a middle-aged man who had many serious health problems. Diagnosed with lung cancer in 2003, Carl had undergone chemotherapy and surgery. He also suffered from diabetes, asthma, and congestive heart failure. Because of his poor health, Carl had not been able to work for 20 years. Adding to his difficulties—or perhaps because of them—when we met him in 2008, Carl told us he had a serious drinking problem and had recently started using cocaine.

Carl had his first child when he was 18; his five adult children all lived in the Chicago area. Harry, his youngest, was just 13 when his mother died, leaving Carl to raise him alone. Harry had his own set of serious mental and physical health challenges; he was autistic and obese. Father and son were close, and during our interviews in 2008 and 2011, Carl spoke candidly about how taking care of Harry had affected his life.

> If his mama would have been living, he would have been there and I would have been free. But now since he is here with me, so I—had to change all my lifestyle around, you know, my going out and like that, you know. I gotta be here with him. So, he slowed me down in a way.

Harry could not read or write well, had trouble communicating, and said other kids picked on him at school. Carl told us he worried constantly about his son and often wondered what would happen to Harry if he died. Carl's main hope was that he would live long enough to see Harry graduate from high school and move into an independent living program.

Like Carl, Erica had failed to qualify for either a voucher or mixed-income housing. When Wells closed, she and her two teenaged daughters moved to one of CHA's rehabbed public housing developments. When I first met Erica in 2008, she was sullen, uncommunicative, and seemed to be high. She had been sleeping when we arrived and made clear she was only cooperating with the

Photo 4.1 Boarded up units in Wells with VPN covers designed to keep out squatters.
Source: Photo by Megan Gallagher.

interview in order to get the $40 incentive. In contrast, her 13-year-old daughter Jasmine was delighted to talk to my colleague. She said she was happy to get away from the shooting and gang violence in Wells. Even though she said there were some problems with rival gangs who had moved from different CHA properties to her new development, she felt much safer. She was also happy to have what she saw as a permanent home—she said her family had moved frequently and that her mother had spent some time in jail. Still, Jasmine said she was doing well in school and was a cheerleader and on the color guard. She had dreams of graduating high school and opening her own hair salon.

NICOLE AND DONITA—THE TOLL OF
TRAUMA AND SUBSTANCE ABUSE

Nicole and Donita represent the other category of "hard to house" residents— single adults, many struggling with drug addiction and significant mental health problems. Nicole was living in the Dearborn Homes when I met her in 2008. She was a long-time drug addict who had lived in the Robert Taylor Homes before CHA closed that development. Like other troubled residents, the CHA had moved her to Dearborn, a smaller development that was serving as a "relocation resource," because she was classified as "working to meet" the criteria for permanent replacement housing. Nicole was so high on heroin when I interviewed her that I could barely follow her story as she told me about her history of childhood sex abuse and trauma. She had her "works" scattered around her dining room table, and her brother was passed out on a chair in her living room, never moving throughout the whole hour we were in her apartment. She told me that her adult children lived nearby and said her grandchildren and her favorite TV preacher were motivating her to think about getting clean. She knew that there were new services, including a substance abuse support group now available in Dearborn, but had not yet mustered up the courage to ask for help.

Like Nicole, Donita was a middle-aged woman grappling with major mental health and substance abuse problems. A long-time Wells resident, she was one of the residents with a big electric bill and knew she faced limited options for replacement housing. Growing up in CHA housing, she had witnessed and experienced a number of traumatic events. Her sister and her close friend were both raped as teenagers; these experiences left her sister mentally ill, disabled, and dependent on Donita for emotional support. Donita herself began drinking and using drugs in high school. But when I met her in 2008, she told me that despite these problems, she managed to graduate and had worked off and on throughout her adult life. As she got older, she developed serious health problems including major depression, asthma, hypertension, and emphysema; she lost many of her teeth because she could not afford the dental work. Her ongoing substance abuse problems contributed to memory loss. Her health made it difficult for her to keep a job. Worst of all, she tearfully admitted that that she was barred from having any contact with her six-year-old son, a situation that left her deeply ashamed and depressed.

RESIDENTS AT RISK

My concern about the "hard to house" grew out of my, by then, more than 15 years of listening to the stories of CHA residents. Our research on the 198 families we were following from Wells and Madden Park as the Plan unfolded reinforced my conviction that it was time to face the fact that better housing alone was not going to be enough to truly help bring these families relief from the instability and ongoing trauma. When we began the Panel study in 2001, it was clear that the CHA and its partners were still overwhelmed with the complexities of moving the massive transformation effort forward at all and were frankly unprepared to engage in a discussion of providing any but the most basic level of resident services.

As the Plan moved forward, one of the roles that I and my team at the Urban Institute played was calling attention to the issue of the urgent need for real supportive services for CHA's large number of vulnerable families. As I described in Chapter 2, in 2002, we were able to get the Ford Foundation to fund a special add-on to our research in Wells and Madden that we called the "Residents at Risk" study. We conducted an additional survey—a census of the whole community as opposed to the Panel Study that was tracking a random sample of 198 households.[2] Finally, as always, we also conducted in-depth interviews with a smaller number of residents in order to understand the complexity of their situations. The goal was to find out how many leasehold-ers were at risk of not being able to "cure" their lease violations and might be losing their right to replacement housing. These lease violations included problems such as: people living in the unit who were not on the lease; peo-ple living in the unit who had criminal records that could disqualify them from living in public housing; and owing back rent or utility payments. The problems were not hard to find; the stories I recall include an older woman with major health problems whose adult son had moved in with her to care for her. They had two problems—he was not on her lease and, because there were so many vacant units in their building, they had simply moved into the two-bedroom apartment next door without permission. Another woman's lease violation was taking in her infant nephew—his parents were drug addicts—and not notifying the property manager. Almost everyone we spoke to had accrued enormous electric bills, sometimes running into thousands of dollars. Electricity was the only utility that tenants had to pay for directly and many had not kept up with their payments, a situation the electric company had apparently allowed to go on for years. But now the utility had begun imposing late fees, which compounded monthly, leaving tenants with enormous bills they had no hope of paying. Until they were able to negotiate a payment plan, this bad debt could leave them ineligible for a permanent relocation choice, including the new mixed-income housing or a voucher.

We continued to follow the 198 Panel Study households, returning to sur-vey both those still on site and those who had moved in 2003. Even though the CHA had begun phased redevelopment in Wells and Madden by that point, we were alarmed to find that only about a third of them had actually managed to leave. The rest were still living on the property, either in an older section of the development that CHA was slowly emptying out or moved to a temporary unit in a building—mainly the high-rises on the north side of the development—slated for demolition in a later phase. This situation under-scored the urgency of quickly putting in place better supports to help these troubled families successfully transition to new and better housing.

Based on both our Panel survey and the Residents at Risk study, we estimated that at least two-thirds of the households in Wells and Madden were "hard to house" and would need much more help and support during the transition than the CHA was then prepared to provide.[3] Some needed this help because of their age or disability, others because they had large households and would have trouble finding a big enough apartment, some had bad debts, and many had mental health or substance abuse problems that made them unattractive tenants.

Our follow-up survey in Wells in 2005 provided more evidence of the need for urgent action—five years after CHA received its HOPE VI grant for Wells and Madden, two-thirds of the families we were tracking were still living on the property. The redevelopment was moving forward, and those families were going to have to move somewhere else—and soon. Conditions in the remaining buildings in Wells were becoming increasingly perilous as vacancy rates rose, the building systems—plumbing, heat, electricity—failed, and CHA struggled to continue to provide basic services. I vividly remember arriving to interview families in the winter of 2006 and finding that no one had shoveled the walks, leaving elderly and disabled tenants trapped inside their apartments. On top of the deteriorating physical conditions and spotty maintenance, the development was becoming increasingly dangerous. As the CHA moved forward with closing the high-rises in Robert Taylor and

Photo 4.2 Ida B. Wells extension. Source: Photo by Megan Gallagher.

Stateway Gardens, displaced gangs and drug dealers moved into Wells and engaged in violent battles over who would control the new territory.

Conditions were almost as bad in the Dearborn and Ickes Homes—the last of the developments that had made up the State Street Corridor, the four-mile stretch of high-rise public housing that was broken up only by the campus of the Illinois Institute of Technology. Dearborn and Ickes were both small high-rise developments by CHA standards—800 and 700 units, respectively—in buildings that were six to nine stories high. The CHA had been using both developments as "relocation resources" for residents from Robert Taylor, Henry Horner, and Stateway Gardens. Dearborn was now home to a mix of long-term tenants and new troubled residents like Nicole who needed a temporary home while they worked to "cure" lease violations that made them ineligible for permanent replacement housing. Making the situation worse was that, as in Wells, displaced drug dealers from the big high-rise developments were now competing for turf. The CHA and the City had a redevelopment plan for Ickes, but no specific plan for Dearborn, leaving residents there with no timeline for when their situation might change.

A SOLUTION FOR THE HARD TO HOUSE

The need for a solution that would protect the troubled families still living in places like Wells and Dearborn from being left behind as the Plan for Transformation progressed led me in a direction I could never have predicted. I began a collaboration with the CHA that has now lasted for more than a decade, working with agency staff and partners from local social service agencies to develop and test improved service models to better meet the needs of public housing families. The model we began to design in 2005 as part of our small research demonstration eventually became the basis of the agency's FamilyWorks program and helped the CHA become a national leader in using its housing as a platform to deliver services to residents.

As I discussed in Chapter 2, during the first five years of implementing the Plan, the CHA and its key partners—especially the City and the MacArthur Foundation—resisted taking on the additional responsibility of providing case management and mental health services. Carrying out the real estate and financial aspects of the Plan was truly daunting and required the team's full attention. With this reality, the team limited its focus on resident services to figuring out a workable relocation system that would ensure that the agency was at least complying with the legal requirements of the Relocation Rights Contract CHA had signed with its resident council.[4] Because of the legacy of the Gautreaux litigation, these services also included "mobility counseling" to help families access to "opportunity neighborhoods" would, in theory, provide adults with access to jobs and children with access to better schools. There were similar hopes about the new mixed-income communities—that living among higher-income neighbors would provide both role models and connections to employers.[5]

The federal policymakers overseeing the CHA's progress on its HOPE VI grants and the Plan for Transformation were not pushing for expanded social services either. Much of the funding for the Plan came from the CHA's many HOPE VI grants, all of which included funding for supportive services. But HUD staff had little experience in providing oversight for public housing authorities' resident services, and they were grappling with their own steep learning curve.[6] And in Chicago, HUD was far more concerned about the CHA's halting progress on demolition, relocation, and new construction than about its failure to deliver on resident services.

Finally, there was the basic reality that neither federal nor local policymakers, including then-Executive Director Terry Peterson, thought providing social services was an appropriate role for a housing authority. When HUD returned the CHA to local control, part of the deal was that the CHA would have Moving to Work (MTW) MTW status, which allowed the agency greater flexibility with its funds. With this flexibility, the CHA could combine its HOPE VI dollars with other funds to pay for expanded resident services if it chose to do so.[7] The City and the MacArthur Foundation brought in the Chicago Department of Human Services (CDHS) to take charge of the resident services. The CHA passed its funds through the CDHS, which contracted directly with service providers for the "Service Connector program." Service Connector agencies were supposed to be on-site in each development, linking residents to services to help them address lease compliance issues that might interfere with their ability to qualify for permanent replacement housing, that is, relocate with a voucher or move to the new mixed-income housing. But initially, the funding was low and caseloads were extremely high—at one point as high as 300 to 1. Under those circumstances, most of Chicago's experienced social service providers were unwilling to participate, and the Service Connector rapidly proved inadequate to meet the level of need. As I described in Chapter 2, an alliance of (usually warring) legal advocacy organizations banded together and sued the CHA over the failures of the relocation system and the Service Connector.[8]

This lawsuit set in motion a process that would take Chicago down a path that was very different from the one that public housing transformation followed in most other cities. The engagement of the Mayor and the MacArthur Foundation meant that there was intense pressure to improve the situation quickly and especially to ensure that leaseholders were not "lost" and denied their right to replacement housing. The Court appointed a special monitor; MacArthur provided the funding for his activities. Further, the Foundation

leadership called regular meetings to discuss progress, problems, and sometimes research results. The CHA focused first on improving its relocation
process, ensuring that residents understood their rights and their choices for
replacement housing. The CHA and CDHS focused on recruiting a new set
of service partners to handle relocation, including Housing Choice Partners
(HCP), which had been providing mobility counseling services for the Cook
County Housing Authority for many years.

Next, CDHS focused on fixing the problems with the Service Connector,
including increasing the funding available to gradually bring caseloads to a
more manageable level, first 150 to 1 and eventually 55 to 1. At the same
time, CDHS reached out to experienced agencies with the capacity to provide high-quality services.[9] Heartland Human Care Services (Heartland) was
one of the well-respected providers that decided to take the risk. Heartland
was a large multiservice agency that had extensive experience in providing
transitional assistance to the homeless and in resettling refugee populations.
As Mary Howard, the service director at Heartland at the time, told the story:

> In 2003–2004, they realized Service Connector in the way they envisioned it
> wasn't working so they did a request to try it again and at that time we bid on it.
> More so with the conviction that while this was happening to this population …
> [CHA residents] didn't have a choice, that we felt strongly that we should inter-
> vene as much as possible and that we should do it with care with other agencies.
> It was an organizational decision to get involved and not stand by despite the
> fact that it was not our core focus. That is when we first started working with
> families in Wells and Lake Park Place.[10]

Finally, the CHA maintained its focus on using the opportunity of the Plan
for Transformation to push its families toward self-sufficiency. Using its
MTW authority, the CHA began talking about imposing work requirements
for its tenants, both those moving into the new mixed-income housing and
those remaining in its traditional public housing developments. The City
created a citywide public-private partnership called "Opportunity Chicago,"
which aimed to help place 5,000 CHA residents in jobs.[11] As described
in Chapter 2, MacArthur spearheaded a consortium of local funders, the
Partnership for New Communities, to support and oversee the effort. In this
context, I, along with other observers, became increasingly concerned about
the need to help support residents in being lease compliant and avoiding losing their right to replacement housing altogether.

In 2005, with the pieces of its service system in place, the leadership
at CHA, the City, and MacArthur became more open to considering new
options, including taking on the problem of finding some kind of case management or supportive housing solution for the most vulnerable families.
They were willing to sit down with us and begin discussing the possibility

of partnering on a research demonstration that would test the feasibility and effectiveness of the CHA's contractors providing intensive case management to these households. With MacArthur and the Casey Foundation providing funds for planning and a group that included our team from Urban Institute, Mary Howard from Heartland, and representatives from HCP and BPI worked to develop a service plan. Howard drew on her and Heartland's expertise to design a service model that was modeled on Heartland's Transitional Assistance to the homeless, and HCP developed a plan for enhanced relocation and mobility services. The goal was that providers from the two agencies would work in partnership to ensure that families got intensive support before and after relocation.

After 12 months of planning and sometimes intense negotiations, the CHA leadership agreed to allow us to move forward with a Demonstration that would target approximately 475 CHA households: all of the remaining residents in Wells and the Dearborn Homes. Heartland and HCP were already the providers for the two developments, which meant that we would be able to build on their existing contracts with CHA. MacArthur and Casey provided additional funds for enhanced services and for the Urban Institute's evaluation and the Demonstration launched in 2007. The CHA had one final stipulation before allowing us to move forward—we were not allowed to call it the Hard to House Demonstration because, as the then-director of resident services pointed out, CHA residents *had* housing. We agreed to use the notably less catchy—but descriptive–"Chicago Family Case Management Demonstration," and the project moved forward.

THE CHICAGO FAMILY CASE MANAGEMENT DEMONSTRATION

The Chicago Family Case Management Demonstration officially ran from 2007 to 2010. One of the first things that happened after CHA leadership approved the project was that Executive Director Terry Peterson, who had led the CHA through most the first six years of the Plan, resigned, as did his director of Resident Services. Sharon Gist-Gilliam, the CHA's Board Chair, stepped in temporarily, replaced about a year later by Lewis Jordan. As part of the transition, the CHA brought in the City's director of Workforce services to head the expanded Resident Services Department. Each change in CHA's leadership meant sometimes delicate negotiations about maintaining the funding and flexibility that were essential for the Demonstration.

The Demonstration offered the residents in Wells and Dearborn an array of services, including intensive case management, clinical mental health counseling ("wellness counselors"), transitional jobs, financial literacy workshops and a matched savings program, substance abuse treatment, and enhanced mobility counseling. HCP's staff offered a set of workshops and lowered the caseloads for its relocation counselors. Engagement rates for the Service Connector hovered around 50 percent, and case managers had such high caseloads—55 to 1—that they were realistically only able to work with those who came into the office to ask for help. The extra funding for the Demonstration services provided meant that we could cut caseloads in half to 25 to 1, leaving time for case managers to do outreach to all of their assigned families and to try to see them at least four times a month. Mary Howard trained her staff in using a "strength-based" approach and using techniques like motivational interviewing rather than focusing strictly on lease compliance. The Urban Institute team's role was to both coordinate the project and provide ongoing evaluation: conducting a baseline and follow-up survey of participants; making regular visits to both sites to observe activities and interview staff; and collecting administrative data to monitor engagement and participation in services. We provided regular feedback to the service team, allowing them to make improvements and mid-course corrections throughout the duration of the project. The experience of having such a hands-on, collaborative role was new to me and my team and fundamentally changed the way that I engaged with the CHA and other housing authorities around, making my research both useful and relevant.

Increasing engagement rates proved to be the easiest part of the work. Heartland increased the number of staff in Dearborn and Wells, as well as assigning more experienced case managers to the teams. In both sites, engagement rates rose rapidly to about 90 percent—and stayed that high for the three years of the project. But it quickly became clear that the work was much harder on staff than our group of planners had anticipated. Our hope was that with lower caseloads, case managers would be less stressed and be able to do a better job. But the reality was that while the lower caseloads mean staff had the time to really get to know their clients, nearly all of them were families with deep and complex problems. The staff uncovered one tough problem after another: residents with schizophrenia who had stopped taking their medications and refused to open the door; women suffering from severe depression; appalling instances of domestic violence; and substance abusers so in debt to drug dealers that the dealers had taken over their apartments. It quickly became apparent that the case managers themselves needed additional support in order to be able to deliver high-quality services.

To address this problem, Mary Howard brought in an experienced social worker to provide regular clinical consultation for the case managers. When we interviewed this clinical director in 2009, she reflected on the challenges of working with this extremely needy population, saying, "This population, from my opinion, is much more vulnerable than the rest of the CHA

Photo 4.3 Dearborn Homes before the buildings were rehabilitated. Source: Photo by Susan Popkin.

population. There is a much higher clinical need … and it's a much harder to reach population." Likewise, Heartland had a substance abuse outreach coordinator in Dearborn who ran a support group for residents and helped link them to drug treatment services. He described his work as extremely challenging because so many women were struggling with a complex mix of mental health and substance use disorders. As he put it:

> Biggest challenge I think is post-traumatic stress disorder. I think in an environment like this, it is very prevalent and it's not being addressed. As a counselor with some clinical background and therapeutic values, you have to be able to work around that … And at least 95 percent of my caseload are females. And when I talk to them about their substance abuse issues and they tell me when it started … it's mostly "That I witnessed my son getting killed," "I was raped." … You know, and I know they've never had any grief counseling or anything like that. You know they just went up went along with their normal life.

Nicole, whose story I introduced earlier in this chapter, was one of the women that the substance abuse counselor was trying hard to help. When I first met her in Dearborn in 2008, she told me that he kept asking her to come to his support group, that she just wasn't ready yet, but thought she would be soon. Underscoring his dedication, the counselor showed up at her door as I was getting ready to leave to invite her once again.

We were fortunate that a year into the Demonstration, the CHA reconfigured its resident services, opening up a new opportunity to expand on-site mental health services. Under the new resident services director, the agency decided to end its arrangement with CDHS and oversee its contracting directly. Further, the Resident Service director was so impressed with Heartland's performance and the resulting high levels of engagement that she decided to incorporate elements of the Demonstration model into the new FamilyWorks program that she was creating to replace the Service Connector.[12] FamilyWorks, as the name implied, was going to emphasize self-sufficiency, and CHA planned to introduce a work requirement that would eventually mean that all adults 18 or over had to be in school, working, or engaging in community service in order for the household to remain lease compliant.[13] All of this happened before we had a chance to show whether or not the more intensive approach actually "worked," i.e., led to better outcomes for families.

The shift from the Service Connector to FamilyWorks meant that Heartland and the CHA's other service providers had to negotiate new contracts in 2008. In Heartland's case, the new contract meant the agency had more resources for the on-site mental health services at both Wells and Dearborn. CHA even provided enough resources that, for a time, Heartland was able to pay for a psychiatrist who came to each site for a few hours a week.[14] To address the high level of serious physical health problems, Heartland also partnered with a local hospital to arrange for a visiting nurse to come to the sites and provided periodic health screenings, such as checking blood pressures.

While CHA's overall expansion of its resident services brought new resources and support for the Demonstration, the agency's continuously shifting redevelopment plans created unexpected challenges. When we launched Demonstration in 2007, we expected that both developments would remain open for the next three years, with relocation in Wells occurring gradually. The plan was that HCP would have enough time to work with families to not only prepare them for relocation, but also encourage them to consider moving to "opportunity areas." But the conditions in Wells were becoming untenable; the pipes in one building burst in the middle of winter, leaving residents with no heat and ice-covered ramps. HCP had to relocate those families on an emergency basis, meaning that there was no opportunity to help them make informed choices about their replacement housing. At the same time, the problems with gangs and drug trafficking were intensifying— I recall visiting Wells in 2007 with a group consisting of our funders and housing activists from the United Kingdom and learning it was too dangerous for us *to even drive* through sections of the development.[15] Faced with this deteriorating situation, the CHA made the decision to quickly close all the remaining buildings in Wells. One consequence was that, as I discussed in Chapter 3, nearly all of the families ended up in what they viewed as better housing in safer neighborhoods, but only a handful ended up moving to lower-poverty, opportunity areas. Another consequence was that Heartland's case managers had to adapt their services from an on-site model to one where they followed families who were now scattered across the city, some with vouchers and others in the remaining traditional public housing developments.

The situation in Dearborn was not as chaotic, but virtually all of the families there also ended up having to move during the course of the Demonstration. HUD awarded the CHA a relatively small HOPE VI rehabilitation grant for Dearborn—$8 million as compared to the $35 million the agency received for the Wells and Madden redevelopment. The CHA would not demolish and replace Dearborn with mixed-income housing, but rather proposed to gut all of the buildings and refurbish the units. Like some of CHA's smaller developments—Wentworth Gardens, Trumbull Park, and Lowden Homes—Dearborn would remain a traditional public housing community, with residents hopefully benefitting from neighborhood improvements generated by the redevelopment activities at Ickes and Stateway Gardens. All of the remaining residents at Dearborn would have to move, but many would be able to simply move directly into a new apartment in a refurbished building. Still, the case managers at Dearborn also ended up having to adapt their services to follow the comparatively small number of residents who moved to different communities across Chicago.

HOW WELL DID IT WORK?

The first big question for the Demonstration was whether even this extra investment of resources and using a more intensive approach to case management would be enough to support these very vulnerable families through the relocation process. An even bigger unknown was whether this investment would help improve their circumstances in the longer term—would it keep them from becoming homeless, help stabilize their mental health, help parents re-engage with the labor market, and help children fare better in school and avoid risky behavior? In more pragmatic terms, was this investment cost-effective and would it have a long-term payoff both for the families and for the CHA and other systems—health care, criminal justice, education, etc.?

Because we were coordinating the project and monitoring program activities, we knew early on that the Demonstration was succeeding on many levels. Heartland and HCP had managed to implement and continue to refine the enhanced services. Heartland case managers had engaged 90 percent of the families they had targeted, and Heartland had added clinical support for both the families and its own case managers. Staff turnover was low, and case managers had formed long-term relationships with their clients. As noted above, CHA's Resident Services director was already so impressed that she had decided to replace the Service Connector with a new model, FamilyWorks, which included elements of the Demonstration's enhanced services including the on-site clinicians. She even hired Mary Howard to direct the new FamilyWorks program, allowing her to apply her expertise across all of CHA's family properties. Finally, we knew that Heartland had been able to continuously adapt and improve its services to reflect the staff's experience on the ground. For example, the team had uncovered extremely low literacy levels among participants in the transitional jobs program and had added literacy services. But we still did not know whether or how these services were actually changing outcomes for the families who were the intended beneficiaries.

To find out the answer to these questions, we conducted a follow-up survey of the participants in 2009. Given that the Demonstration intentionally targeted high-need CHA families who had failed to qualify for mixed-income housing or vouchers, there was ample reason to expect that even high-quality intensive services might have only modest effects at best. Even if we saw good results after two years, there was no guarantee that these gains would last, especially as the extra resources for intensive services ended after 2010. So we followed up with the Demonstration families again in 2011 when we also conducted our 10-year follow-up survey of the Chicago Panel Study participants—we called the combined study the Long-Term Outcomes Study for CHA Families.

We were pleasantly surprised to find evidence in from these two follow-up surveys that not only did Demonstration participants benefit in many ways but that these changes lasted even after the intensive services ended. Further, Demonstration participants fared better in many ways than the residents we followed as part of the Chicago Panel Study, who only got CHA's regular Service Connector and relocation services. The additional costs for intensive services were relatively modest, suggesting that it might be feasible to take this model to scale.[16]

SUCCESSFUL RELOCATION

One major achievement was that, despite the fact that the CHA's changing redevelopment and relocation plans had a major impact on Demonstration participants and services, the majority of these families ended up in better housing in safer neighborhoods—just like their less-troubled counterparts in the CHA Panel Study. Since I've already covered this issue in Chapter 3, I am not going to spend a great deal of time on it here. But it is worth noting that Demonstration participants were targeted for the intensive services precisely *because they had not qualified for permanent replacement housing.* The only major difference between them and the Panel Study households was that, because so many Dearborn residents moved directly into a rehabbed apartment in a different building, more than half of the Demonstration participants (59 percent) stayed in traditional public housing. In contrast, Panel respondents were most likely to have moved to the private market with a voucher. Surprisingly, when we surveyed both groups in 2011, those in the rehabbed public housing units in Dearborn and elsewhere reported better housing conditions and fewer problems with crime and disorder on average than voucher holders.[17] Another surprise was that Demonstration participants were nearly as likely as those in the Panel Study to end up in the new mixed-income housing—13 percent vs. 18 percent, respectively. We had thought it was unlikely that *any* Demonstration participants would be able to meet the stringent criteria—strict work requirements and annual drug testing—that came with moving into the new developments.

Many of the families I've introduced throughout this book were Demonstration participants and most ended up in better circumstances. In Chapter 3, Joyce and her grandchildren who moved to an opportunity neighborhood on the north side were hard to house participants, as were Sharon and Jamie who were so happy in their townhouse in Englewood. Carl and his son introduced earlier in this chapter were struggling in many ways but were content in their refurbished unit in the smaller public housing community on the far south side. Erica and her daughter felt safer in their new development. Nicole and Donita both stayed in public housing, both in refurbished units in safer developments. But there were also families who struggled like Annette and her children; as I've shown, that family floundered once they left public housing and the easy access to services and supports. I will return to their story in the next chapter when I discuss how the Demonstration results led us to think about how to try to modify the model with a more intentional focus on serving children and youth.

MODEST INCREASES IN EMPLOYMENT

Beyond the housing outcomes, we found that "Hard to House" participants were more likely to be working after receiving the intensive services, which included the transitional jobs program. These gains in employment occurred despite the extremely tough labor market in 2008–2010, the height of the Great Recession. And they also occurred despite the fact that public housing residents in general face numerous barriers to employment, including: low educational attainment; poor mental and physical health; limited access to social networks that facilitate job access; and physical isolation from opportunity. There have been a number of efforts over the years to address these barriers and improve self-sufficiency, but only the Jobs Plus program, which saturated public housing communities with on-site employment services, showed any impact.[18] So the fact that the combination of intensive case management and transitional jobs seemed to help the Demonstration participants was an unexpected success.

The intensive services for the Demonstration ended in mid-2010, at about the same time the CHA began scaling back its citywide Transitional Jobs program that was part of Opportunity Chicago. We were concerned that the employment gains we saw in 2009 might fade quickly.[19] But when we followed up with the Demonstration participants again in 2011, we found that they had held, especially for those who had moved to traditional public housing. More than half (51 percent) of participants under age 62 reported current employment, up 18 percentage points from 33 percent in 2007; approximately 70 percent reported being employed in the last year, a more than 20 percentage point increase from 45 percent when the Demonstration began in 2007.[20]

DEMONSTRATION SERVICES LEAD
TO IMPROVED HEALTH

Over the years that I've surveyed public housing residents, I've consistently found that they report dramatically worse physical and mental health than most other Americans—even other poor Americans—and that bad health contributes to their low rates of employment. Further, as we followed residents over time for the five-city HOPEVI Panel Study (which included Wells), we found that their health continued to deteriorate over time, even after they moved to better circumstances.[21] In Chicago, when we first surveyed the Panel Study participants from Wells in 2001, about a third of them rated their health as fair or poor; 10 years later, that figure had risen to 48 percent.

Given these other research findings, I had no reason to expect that the "Hard to House" Demonstration participants would fare any better, and in fact, thought that it was likely that, given their many challenges, they might look even worse. When we first talked to them in 2007, they did: more than half (53 percent) rated their health as fair or poor. But when we followed up with them two years later, the proportion reporting poor health had declined slightly, and when we talked to them again in 2011, it had decreased to 38 percent. So, to our surprise, after three years of intensive services, the Demonstration participants were rating their health better than their counterparts in the Panel Study.[22]

But it is important to remember that even with this impressive and surprising improvement, Demonstration participants were hardly in good shape. They were still three times more likely to report poor health than the general adult population and even more likely than other poor adults (28 percent of whom report poor health).[23] Like the Panel Study respondents, their rates of chronic illness, including hypertension, diabetes, heart disease, and obesity, remained extremely high, and about half were regular smokers. Underscoring the severity of their health problems, mortality rates for both Demonstration participants and Panel participants were shockingly high; between 2007 and 2011, six percent of the Demonstration sample had died, a rate twice that expected for the general population (three percent) and 50 percent higher than for African-American women (four percent).[24,25]

Our evaluation also showed that effort to provide on-site clinical mental health services seemed to have had important benefits—and may have contributed to the improvements we saw in health and employment. When we first followed up with Demonstration participants after two years, we found the first positive sign: their rates of worry and anxiety had decreased. And as was the case with physical health, when we talked to them again in 2011—a year after the intensive services ended—we found even better news. The proportion reporting worry and anxiety had continued to drop and, more significantly, Demonstration participants were increasingly less likely to report symptoms of depression in 2011 (11 percent) than in 2007 (17 percent).[26] The reduction in depression was greatest among participants who relocated to traditional public housing, perhaps because that meant they still had access to CHA's FamilyWorks clinical providers.[27] In contrast, as was the case with physical health, the residents we tracked for the CHA Panel Study were worse off in 2011 than when we first surveyed them, reporting higher levels of depression and worry than they did in 2001.

The question we had to answer was: Why did the Demonstration participants get better? Was it simply because they finally were able to leave the terrible conditions they were living in Wells and Dearborn in 2007? Or was it a result of the Demonstration services? Our evaluation was not a random control trial, so we cannot know for certain, but it appears from the analyses we were able to do that the participants' mental and physical health improved primarily because of the intensive services. Moving to safer neighborhoods helped, too, but not as much as the attention they received from Heartland's case managers.[28]

Photo 4.4 Dearborn Homes after rehab. Source: Photo by Susan Popkin.

HARD TO HOUSE FAMILIES BENEFIT

Erica and her daughters were one of the families that truly benefitted from
the intensive services the Demonstration provided. After several years of
intensive help from Heartland case managers prior to and after moving from
Wells, Erica's situation stabilized. When we talked to Erica and Jasmine
again in 2011, Erica, who had been high and uncommunicative when I met
her in 2008, was now working for FamilyWorks, both in the summer feeding
program and doing janitorial work. She said that moving to the new development was a key step to stabilizing—she had help, she had a job, she joined
the tenant patrol, and she was even thinking about running for the resident
council. Jasmine and her sister were also doing well. When we talked to her
again in 2011, Jasmine was starting her junior year and was enrolled in the
cosmetology program. She continued to love to do hair, and she had income
from that as well. She was on track to receive her cosmetology license upon
graduating from high school. When we asked Erica where she saw herself in
five years, she said living in the same place, but with a better job. She had
even bigger dreams for the future:

In the next ten years, I'll own a house. I'm getting, I won't be here for long. I already know. This is just to help me save money because we only pay rent here, no light, no gas, no water, no nothing, just rent.

Nicole, who I introduced earlier in this chapter, was another success story—albeit a more modest one. When I met her in 2009, Heartland's substance abuse counselor was working hard to get Nicole to come to his support group and get help for her heroin addiction. At that point, Nicole was wavering, but he was remarkably persistent. In the short time I was in Dearborn that day, I saw him come to her door and then talk to her again when she came outside later on. When we saw her in 2011, she told us he had helped her get into detox, although Nicole confided that she had experienced relapses, and it appeared that her struggle with the drug was ongoing. In addition, he had helped her find a job working part-time in food services, which allowed Nicole to be more self-sufficient. Nicole also said she saw her three adult children and grandchildren frequently and felt that the changes in Dearborn had improved her quality of life. She told us her building was cleaner and safer and said she was able to walk around her development without being harassed.

Carl and his son Harry were also a qualified success story. When we went back to see them in 2011, Carl still worried a great deal about how Harry would be able to function without his support, and their family situation remained challenging. But they were content with their housing, Carl's health was relatively stable, and Harry had managed to finish high school and was planning to move onto college.

Donita, the woman with combination of physical and mental health problems and a history of substance abuse so severe that she had been barred from contact with her only child, was faring less well. She was stable in her public housing apartment and still getting help from CHA's FamilyWorks case managers. But even with Heartland's help, she was unable to find another job and she did not qualify for disability. In 2011, she was surviving on SNAP benefits and help from her sister, who was on Supplemental Security Income (SSI). Her days were consumed by traveling from one free clinic or pharmacy to another to get her medications. Her case manager could do little more than offer encouragement and provide her with transportation vouchers to get to her appointments.

Sadly, even though Annette received a great deal of support from her case manager before and after she moved out of Wells to her private market apartment, her family was in dire straits. When I met Annette in 2008, she and her children were living in miserable conditions with almost no furniture in their home—I sat on the only chair to conduct our interview. Annette said she went back to the Heartland office regularly to talk to her case manager and try to resolve her problems, but she was clearly in crisis. Both she and her son were so dangerously depressed that we did something I have rarely done in my years as a researcher and broke confidentiality in order to be able to get them immediate assistance. Fortunately, at that point, the Demonstration was still ongoing, and we were able to contact her case manager to come and try to help stabilize the situation. She did—and also showed us photos of all the furniture they'd provided when they helped Annette move, all of it now presumably sold to buy drugs. I don't know whether this intervention helped stabilize the situation for a while or was just another failed crisis intervention, but I do know that when we went back in 2011, the family was once again in crisis, and we ended up once again breaking confidentiality and calling for help, this time for Annette and her daughter. I remain glad that CHA's by-then very robust Resident Services meant there was someone to call, but also painfully aware of the reality that it would take something far more intensive—perhaps family supportive housing—to really help stabilize a family this troubled.

A QUALIFIED SUCCESS STORY

The Chicago Family Case Management/Hard to House Demonstration was a success on many levels. First, it represented the CHA's entry into a new, expanded commitment to resident services and an openness to experimenting with different models and approaches. Before we'd even gotten halfway through our evaluation, CHA's leadership had already decided to roll out a lighter version of the service model to all of their traditional public housing and mixed-income communities. And as I noted earlier, before the Demonstration ended in 2010, the CHA hired Mary Howard away from Heartland to direct its FamilyWorks program. In 2012, she became the Director of Resident Services overall and, as of this writing, holds the title of Chief Resident Services Officer. CHA also dramatically increased its spending on resident services; by 2010, the agency was spending about $40 million a year on a range of different types of services, including assistance for seniors and programming for its youth. The CHA's large, well-funded Resident Services Department is the envy of many other housing authorities, and Mary Howard is widely recognized as a leader in the field.

Second, the Demonstration was the beginning of the CHA's becoming a real research partner, willing to share data and collaborate with us and other researchers to help understand the implications of its massive experiment with public housing transformation. On a personal note, the experience of developing and collaborating on the Demonstration changed the way that I conduct my work. I am now much more intimately engaged in community-based and "research into action," the kind of formative work that helps inform practice on the ground.

Third and most importantly, this project showed that it was possible for a housing authority to partner with social service agencies to develop a service model that had the potential to truly use housing as a platform to improve residents' lives. The Demonstration service model worked better than we had ever anticipated: case managers were able to engage even some of the hardest-to-reach families, and the combination of intensive case management, transitional jobs, and clinical mental health services changed residents' lives for the better. Participants relocated successfully and saw gains in employment, physical health, anxiety, and depression. But even with these impressive changes, the Hard to House adults who were the target of the Demonstration were still struggling—while better, their health was still poor, their risk of mortality high, and their ability to hold a steady job limited. Further, even the intensive services were not enough to meet the deep needs of families like Donita or Annette's, and there is still a clear need for even more intensive— and expensive—solutions like permanent supportive housing to help ensure that their children do not end up equally troubled and traumatized.

Finally, as I discuss in the next chapter, while the Demonstration succeeded in serving adults in many ways, it was less successful in changing the trajectory for the youth in these households. Building a two-generation strategy to meet the needs of the whole family became the next challenge for us and our partners at the CHA.

NOTES

1. Susan J. Popkin, Mary K. Cunningham, and Martha Burt. "Public Housing Transformation and the Hard to House." 2005. Housing Policy Debate 16 (1): 1–24.

2. We also aimed to survey and count the squatters who were using the development as a defacto homeless shelter—as I discussed in Chapter 2, over a two-week period, we counted nearly 300 adults and 94 children who were squatting in vacant units, hallways, stairwells, and laundry rooms.

3. See Popkin et al. 2005, note 1, and Popkin and Cunningham 2005 "Demolition and Struggle: Public Housing Transformation in Chicago and the Challenges for Residents" in Xavier de Souza Briggs (ed.) Housing Race and Regionalism: Rethinking the Geography of Race in America. Washington, D.C.: Brookings: 176–196.

4. Interview with Terry Peterson, CHA Executive Director 2000–2006 June 5, 2013

5. See Susan J. Popkin, F. Larry. Buron, Diane. K. Levy, and Mary K. Cunningham. 2000. "The Gautreaux Legacy: What Might Mixed-Income and Dispersal Strategies Mean for the Poorest Public Housing Tenants?" *Housing Policy Debate*, 11(4): 911–942; Popkin et al. 2004. *A Decade of HOPE VI* and Robert J. Chaskin and Mark Joseph, 2015, *Integrating the Inner-City.*

6. The HOPE VI legislation that authorized CSS emphasized services that would focus on employment and self-sufficiency rather than case management. The 1990s were the era of welfare reform, HUD was pushing its own transformation efforts to

show that public and assisted housing could be "a platform" to help families improve their economic circumstances.

7. Interview with Terry Peterson, CHA Executive Director 2000–2006 June 5, 2013.

8. Our Residents At Risk study was part of the evidence that advocates used to make the case that the Service Connector model was a failure.

9. Susan J. Popkin. 2010. "A Glass Half-Empty: Public Housing Families in Transition." *Housing Policy Debate* 20(1): 42–62.

10. Interview with Mary Howard, Chicago Housing Authority Chief Resident Services Officer, June 5 2013.

11. For information on Opportunity Chicago and evaluations of the program components, see: http://cjc.net/opportunity-chicago/.

12. For more information, see http://www.thecha.org/pages/case_management_ _familyworks_/31.php and http://www.thecha.org/pages/plans__reports___policies/ 40.php.

13. Public housing residents living in the new mixed-income housing communities are also subject to work requirements, while voucher holders were still exempt as of 2011. For details of the work requirements, see the FY 2009 Admissions and Continued Occupancy Policy (ACOP) and the Minimum Tenant Selection Plan for Mixed-Income/Mixed-Finance Communities (MTSP) at http://www.thecha.org/ pages/plans_reports_policies/40.php.

14. Susan J., Popkin, Brett Theodos, Liza Getsinger, and Joe Parilla. 2010. An Overview of the Chicago Family Case Management Demonstration. Supporting Vulnerable Public Housing Families, Brief No. 1. Washington, DC: The Urban Institute. http://www.urban.org/publications/412254.html.

15. Harris Beider, Diane K. Levy and Susan J. Popkin. 2009. Community Revitalization in the United States and the United Kingdom. Washington, DC: The Urban Institute. http://www.urban.org/research/publication/community-revitalization-united-states-and-united-kingdom.

16. Further analyses suggested strategies for careful targeting to maximize cost-efficiency and impact. See Brett Theodos, Susan J. Popkin, Joe Parilla, and Liza Getsinger. 2012. "The Challenge of Targeting Services: A Typology of Public Housing Residents," *Social Service Review* 86(3): 517–544.

17. Larry Buron, Christopher Hayes and Chantal Hailey. 2013. An Improved Living Environment, but … Washington, DC: The Urban Institute. http://www.urban. org/research/publication/improved-living-environment.

18. Although initiatives that relocate public housing residents to a better neighborhood (such as the Moving to Opportunity demonstration or HOPE VI) appear to improve overall quality of life, they have not affected employment outcomes for adults. See Briggs, Popkin, and Goering 2010; Diane K. Levy. 2010. The Limits of Relocation: Employment and Family Well-Being Among Former Madden/Wells Residents. CHA Families and the Plan for Transformation, Brief No. 6. http://www.urban.org/sites/default/files/alfresco/publication-pdfs/412186-The-Limits-of-Relocation-Employment-and-Family-Well-Being-among-Former-Madden-Wells-Residents.pdf. In contrast, the Jobs-Plus program, which sought to connect public housing residents to employment through employment services,

rent incentives, and community support for work, led to marked gains in resident employment and earnings when properly implemented. See Howard Bloom, James Riccio, and Nandita Verma, 2005. *Promoting Work in Public Housing: The Effectiveness of Jobs Plus.* New York: MDRC. http://www.mdrc.org/publication/promoting-work-public-housing. Also, Project Match, a Chicago-based workforce development program that offered comprehensive employment services, increased earnings for some program participants by 105 percent over 10 years. See Toby Herr and Susan Wagner, 2009, "Labor Economics versus Barriers to Work versus Human Development: Finding the Right Lens for Looking at Labor Force Attachment." In Margery A. Turner, Susan J. Popkin and Lynette Rawlings, *Public Housing and the Legacy of Segregation.* Washington, DC: Urban Institute Press: 221–36.

19. Susan J Popkin and Elizabeth Davies. 2013. Improving the Lives of Public Housing's Most Vulnerable Families. Long-Term Outcomes for CHA Residents, Brief No. 4. Washington, DC: The Urban Institute. http://www.urban.org/publications/412763.html.

20. See Carlos A. Manjarrez, Susan J. Popkin, and Elizabeth Guernsey. 2007. "Poor Health: Adding Insult to Injury for HOPE VI Families." HOPE VI: Where Do We Go from Here? Brief 5. Washington, DC: The Urban Institute. http://www.urban.org/projects/hopevi/index.cfm; David Price and Susan J. Popkin 2010. The Health Crisis for CHA Families. CHA Families and the Plan for Transformation, Brief No. 5. Washington, DC: The Urban Institute. http://www.urban.org/publications/412184.html.; and Popkin and Davies 2013.

21. The change from 2007 to 2011 is statistically significant ($p<0.05$).

22. 2010 National Health Interview survey, age-adjusted summary health statistics for U.S. adults.

23. The mortality rate for the general population is calculated by determining the probability that each respondent would survive based on averages for people of their age and sex using a 2005 National Vital Statistics Reports life table.

24. Attrition analysis revealed that Demonstration respondents who died were also more likely to have had an illness requiring ongoing care and an in ability to work due to health problems and/or a disability that prevents work. They were also more likely to have been older and/or obese, to drink regularly, and to have had multiple health problems. Those who died in the Demonstration sample did not differ from those still living in terms of self-reported health, anxiety, or depression.

25. Depression is measured using the short form of the Composite International Diagnostic Interview (CIDI-SF), a fully-structured interview designed to be administered by lay interviewers who are not necessarily licensed clinicians. For this study, we eliminate two of the seven questions used to develop the CIDI-SF scale in order to compare depression accurately across waves. Our five-item scale is correlated with the seven-item scale at $r=0.99$.

26. Improvements in the neighborhood may also have helped to improve mental health among Demonstration residents, as previous research findings suggest that crime, and fear of crime, is linked to higher levels of anxiety. See Caterina Gouvis Roman and Carly Knight. 2009. *An Examination of the Social and Physical*

Environment of Public Housing Residents in Two Chicago Developments in Transition. Washington, DC: The Urban Institute. http://www.urban.org/research/publication/examination-social-and-physical-environment-public-housing-residents-two-chicago-developments-transition.

27. Susan J. Popkin, Megan Gallagher, Chantal Hailey, Elizabeth Davies, Larry Buron, and Christopher Hayes. 2013. CHA Residents and the Plan for Transformation. Long-Term Outcomes for CHA Residents, Brief No. 2. Washington, DC: The Urban Institute. http://www.urban.org/publications/412761.html.

28. Popkin et al. 2013, note 27.

Chapter Five

Reaching the Next Generation

As I've documented in the previous chapters, the Plan for Transformation led to many positive changes for families, the CHA, and even for the City of Chicago as a whole. Nearly all of the displaced families ended up in better housing in much less dangerous—albeit still poor and racially segregated—neighborhoods. Demolishing the high-rises led to a reduction in violent crime across the city and, just as important, did *not* lead to major crime waves in other neighborhoods. The Plan led to new partnerships like the Chicago Family Case Management Demonstration that showed it was possible to make positive changes for even the most troubled residents and brought high-quality services and resources to CHA's developments. Finally, the experience of implementing the Plan completed the transformation of the CHA itself from the worst housing authority in the United States into a relatively well-functioning city agency, one with a professional Resident Services Department.

With public health advocates claiming affordable housing as a "vaccine" to promote children's health and well-being, it was reasonable to hope—and expect—that children would benefit the most from the CHA's transformation.[1] And there is no question that relocation really did rescue thousands of children from what were then the most dangerous places in Chicago. And yet it seemed to do little to alter their life chances: the children we followed were indeed living in safer places and had better-quality housing, but most did not seem to be doing better in school or managing to avoid risky behavior and the criminal justice system.[2] Our final survey of the families from both the Panel Study and the Demonstration 2011 confirmed the worrying trends we found along the way and led us to conclude that youth who lived through CHA's Plan gained little more than a slightly better quality of life. Other observers also noted that even when they moved to better neighborhoods, these children did not seem to gain access to better schools.[3] In 2011, most young adults were neither in school nor working; most teens were facing academic failure, delinquency, and trauma. We were forced to conclude that the majority of these young people were likely to end up almost as badly off as their parents, living in marginal neighborhoods and cycling in and out of the workforce.[4]

Many of the stories of the young people we got to know through our research reflected this sad reality. I introduced Michelle and her daughter, Tonya, in Chapter 1. Michelle herself was doing relatively well, working steadily and appreciating her apartment in Oakwood Shores, the mixed-income development that replaced the Wells and Madden developments. But over the 10 years we followed her family, her sons got involved in drug dealing and gangs and at least one ended up in prison. And Tonya, who graduated from high school and even started college, got pregnant and had to drop out after less than a year. Likewise, Matthew and his grandchildren had ended up in rehabilitated public housing development after a failed stint in Oakwood Shores. His granddaughter Amara had also managed to graduate from high school with plans to head to college, but also got pregnant and gave up. The last time we saw her, she was neither in school nor working, her son's father was in jail, and, at age six, her son was already exhibiting the kinds of behavior problems that portend major struggles in school. Monique, who I introduced in Chapter 3, was proud of the way that moving out of public housing had changed her own life and pushed her toward self-sufficiency but was disappointed that her older son, who had been doing well in school for a while, had dropped out and become a drug dealer. Jade's daughter, Layla (Chapter 3), started out happy about the quiet and nice neighbors on her block but was profoundly traumatized after a house fire that took the life of her sister and niece. Her sister, Rhonda, was trying hard to do better than her mother but was churning her way through a series of low-wage jobs and had just landed in the Job Corps, hoping it would help her stabilize. Saddest of all were Annette and her children (Chapters 1 and 4): her son, Robert, was lost to the streets by the time he became a teenager; her daughter, Denise, admitted that their situation was desperate enough to drive her to trading sexual favors for money to pay the bills.

Even kids who seemed to be doing well, like Sharon's daughter, Jamie (Chapter 3), and Erica's daughter, Jasmine (Chapter 4), still talked about having to learn to navigate the gangs and drug dealers in their new communities and avoid the violence around them. When we last saw them, Jamie was headed to college, and Jasmine was on track to finish high school. And, as the stories of Joyce's grandchildren John and Maia (Chapter 3) showed, even the few youth whose families moved to low-poverty "opportunity" neighborhoods still struggled, feeling like they had to "watch their backs" and defend themselves from other teens in their community. Both of them talked about getting into fights in school, and Maia dealt drugs for a short period before cleaning up her act when she realized her new school offered her real chances to improve her circumstances.

In this chapter, I tell the story of what happened to the children we followed and try to explain why so many of them struggled even when their parents seemed to benefit. And I also tell the story of how the CHA's Mary Howard and I got the unexpected opportunity in 2010 to begin developing and testing a response to this sad situation. The Housing Opportunities and Services Together or HOST Demonstration is still ongoing and is serving as a laboratory for using housing as a platform for testing "two-generation approaches" that combine services for parents with services for children and youth. It is too soon to tell how successful these efforts will be in the long run, but the HOST experience offers important lessons for understanding the challenges involved in truly improving the life chances for children growing up in deeply poor communities.

FOLLOWING CHA'S CHILDREN

Our information on children's experiences with the Plan from 2001 to 2011 came from two different sources. We did not survey children and youth directly; rather, we asked parents to answer a series of questions about one or two "focal children" per household.[5] The interviewers selected one child under six and one child six to 18 from a list of all of the children in the household, and we tried to ask parents about the same two children each time we interviewed them.[6] Between our initial contacts with families in 2001 and 2007 and our final follow-up survey of all families in 2011, many of these children grew into young adults. In 2011, we collected parent reports about 121 children under 12, 109 teenagers (age 13–17), and 102 young adults (age 18 or older). In addition to these parent reports, we interviewed selected children and youth along with their parents after each round of survey for both the Panel and Demonstration studies—as I noted in Chapter 2, those interviews are the basis for the stories that appear throughout this book.

COMPLICATED CHILDHOODS IN
DISTRESSED NEIGHBORHOODS[7]

It is important to keep in mind that although the families we followed ended up in places that were considerably safer than the Wells and Dearborn developments, most were not living in what anybody would consider a "good neighborhood." For the most part, the communities they moved to were still "chronically disadvantaged": high poverty, racially segregated, and chronically violent—just not as violent as the CHA's developments.[8] It is important to remember that Wells and Dearborn were truly terrible places before CHA redeveloped them. When we first visited Wells in 2001, residents reported terrible conditions: most reported that gangs (75 percent), shootings and violence (69 percent), and drug trafficking (85 percent) were big problems in the community.[9] The situation for the families we interviewed in Dearborn and Wells at the beginning of the Demonstration in 2007 was little better, with the proportion reporting these problems just slightly lower. The places where these families landed by 2011 were better, but still far from ideal: about a quarter of the people we surveyed still reported serious problems with drug trafficking and violent crime.[10] And these communities were very disadvantaged—about 40 percent poor and 87 African-American—again, not as bad as the places where the CHA families came from, but hardly "opportunity neighborhoods."

The children we followed came from families and places that threatened their development and life chances. Researchers have become increasingly aware of the short- and long-term effects of childhood exposure to adverse events like parental dysfunction and community violence. In the short term, youth exposed to high levels of community disorder and violence often become the victims or even perpetrators of violence, exhibiting the same psychological trauma as children growing up in urban war zones.[11] In the long term, higher levels of cumulative childhood exposure to violence predict future physical and mental health problems and emotional distress throughout adulthood.[12] And children growing up with parents struggling with substance abuse, mental health problems, and domestic violence are at even greater risk.[13] We knew from our research, especially on the Demonstration, that these kinds of problems were all too common among CHA families, and that the children in these households were likely to have problems.

Sadly, the effects of growing up in families and neighborhoods with these persistent "toxic stressors" were plainly evident for many of the children and youth we followed from 2001 to 2011: they exhibited high rates of negative and delinquent behaviors, both indicators of poor mental health and well-being. In 2011, parents reported that in the prior year, 19 percent of teenagers and 11 percent of young adults engaged in two or more delinquent behaviors.[14] These figures changed little from when we first interviewed their parents when they lived in Wells and Dearborn in 2001 and 2007. And our statistics include indicators of very serious problems like the 35 percent of teenagers who had been suspended from school, and 20 percent of teenagers and 25 percent of young adults who had some involvement with the criminal justice system (i.e., getting in trouble with the police, being arrested, or going to jail or juvenile court). Since these figures are based on parents' reports, they likely underestimate the true scope of the problems of these CHA youth.

In addition to these disturbingly high rates of reported delinquency and behavior problems, the children and youth we followed were clearly struggling in school. According to their parents, just under half of young children and two-thirds of teenagers were "not highly engaged in school," meaning that they were not performing well academically.[15] Further, more than one in 10 young children and one in three teens were not on track—that is, their age was not appropriate for their grade. Most distressing, a third of young adults were "disconnected," neither working nor in school, a poor indicator for their prospects for success later in adulthood.[16]

Our conversations with teens and young adults in 2011 made clear that even though they had escaped the projects, most still lived in dangerous neighborhoods with high levels of concentrated poverty. In other words, they have not moved far enough to escape the chronic stress and trauma that drove their behavior problems and poor performance in school. Only a few like Joyce and her grandchildren in Chapter 3 have made it to the kinds of lower-poverty places that offer better opportunities for kids. In contrast, most of the families who moved with vouchers ended up in troubled communities on Chicago's west side like Englewood or Garfield Park, and most of the rest

Photo 5.1 Children on playground in Cabrini-Green. Source: Photo by Kyle Higgins.

were living in rehabilitated CHA housing. It is true that by 2011, CHA developments were actually somewhat safer than the private-market neighborhoods where the voucher holders lived because they had on-site security and property management, but, by definition, these communities were extremely high poverty.[17]

When we spoke to them in 2009 and again in 2011, parents and youth talked about having to cope with the violence around them—much as they had when they lived in the projects. Many parents said they still limited their children to playing in their own house or on their own street. One voucher holder told us that neighborhood children played on the roofs of the houses to escape the drug dealers and gang bangers. But even when they tried their best to protect them, it was impossible to completely prevent their children from being exposed to violence and disorder. Adrianne, a mother living with her husband and six children (ages 0 to 16) in a private rental, told us the trauma her kids experienced when they witnessed a group "jumping" a young man:

> There was an incident with the kids, they were playing in the water hydrant, and there was a shooting. They [the perpetrators] shot up in the air, and they were jumping on a guy, and they were stomping him, you know, really violent about it. And the kids were so traumatized by it. They were crying, they were scared. You know, they were like, "Mommy, he's not breathing," "Mommy, they hit him with a bat."

Dionne, a teenager also living in a private-market rental, explained that being exposed to violence is often unavoidable—and terrifying:

> I was at the wrong place at the wrong time. … Next thing you know … they came through the gangway out of somebody else yard and shot this dude. He was on his way upstairs. … He was at the wrong place and the wrong time, shot him and his cousin. The boy, that was the first time I saw somebody get killed. … Like literally got killed. … That like scared me like, come on now. And then I see blood. … That's, I pray to God I don't get shot.

Like Monique and Jade in Chapter 3, residents who answered our survey in 2011 made clear that they were willing to uproot their families repeatedly in search of a place where they could feel safe. A quarter of residents with vouchers who had moved in the past two years said that they chose their new neighborhood because they hoped it was safer or would have fewer problems with gangs or drugs. Key events that occurred in the summer of 2011 may have made families feel more vulnerable; these included the fatal shootings of a sleeping six-year-old girl through her grandmother's window in Englewood and a 13-year-old boy playing basketball at a Bronzeville park near the Dearborn Homes. Kenny, a 15-year-old boy living in one of the refurbished units in Dearborn, was friends with the boy who was killed and witnessed the shooting, leaving both him and his mother, Ginny, traumatized and fearful. Kenny said that when he was younger, his mother did not have to worry so much, but now, she worried all the time:

> When I was younger, she didn't have to worry that much. All she had to worry about was "is he in the house, or … he sleep, and he eat." That's all she had to worry about. Now she got to worry about with all the killing", is he okay …. a police car going past, look."

Kenny referred to himself as a "ghost" in Dearborn, because he didn't hang out with any of the guys—all of his friends lived in Wentworth Gardens, a development about a mile away where his mother grew up. He and Ginny believed he was safe in Wentworth but were worried about his safety near his own building in Dearborn. Still, he said the community was better than it used to be:

> I feel safe. It's a safe environment. I mean, like don't really nothing go on down here. All they do is play basketball, hang out, play with the females. It's safe. It's better than how it used to be … It used to be real bad, from the drugs to the killings. Now you don't see nothing like, all they do, literally, all they do is sit on the court and play basketball. That's why I don't know why the police are still be messing with them.

Some of the residents we interviewed said that things had gotten so bad in Chicago's poor communities that they believed that moving out of the city was the only way to escape the turmoil. It was true that violent crime was way down from its peak in the 1990s, but as these stories make clear, life was still hard in the city's poor, minority neighborhoods. Adrianne said that she was unsure about where she could go to find a safe place for her six children:

> The whole city is crazy right now. There's violence everywhere, the violence is even starting to stretch over into the suburbs. … I'll try to work it over here because there's a little safety here. … I'll probably go real far west. … But I don't know, they'll probably be just as violent. … I pretty much don't know where to go, that's the honest answer right there. I don't know where to go for safety. It's like if you find a safe place, stay there.

VICTIMS AND VICTIMIZERS

The CHA families we followed moved frequently to try to improve their quality of life and find a safer place to raise their children, but this strategy may also have put their children at risk. First, moving itself is traumatic for kids; there is research that links frequent moves to adverse outcomes, including low academic performance (i.e., grade retention and dropping out of school) and poor social functioning.[18] Second, as we heard from parents and young people that we spoke to in 2011, moving to new neighborhoods sometimes created circumstances that meant that youth were more likely to be both victims and perpetrators of violence. Moving meant leaving behind their established and protective social networks; it was especially hard on boys if they came from a place controlled by a gang or crew that had a rivalry with the ones in their new neighborhood.[19] Official crime statistics confirmed that these families were right to be concerned. As part of our public housing and crime study, we found that that former CHA residents were both more likely than other residents in their new communities to be arrested *and* to be victims of crime after relocation.[20]

Teens we spoke to both in 2009 and in 2011 told us about some of the traumatic experiences that underlie the alarming statistics we found about children's school performance and behavior problems. Davon's story illustrates why moving created such serious problems for children and youth, especially young men. He was 16 when we met him in 2011 and had moved with his family from Wells to a neighborhood on the south side of the city. He told us that when he first arrived, other teens in the community saw him as an outsider. Although he was not active in a gang in Wells and, in fact, was involved in both athletics and church activities, the local gang targeted him because of his family. Some of his relatives in Wells had been involved in gang conflicts and had "beefs" with the guys in his new neighborhood. He told us that he was forced to fight to defend himself:

No, they used tried to fight me. ... I wasn't going [to allow them], but, yeah, they just try and fight me ... I don't know. Because I was the new kid on the block, I guess, and the girls liked me. They was jealous ... like, we walk past a block with our shirts off and stuff, but we would be coming from the church. And like grown people that tried to, the grown [gang members], they tried tell us we couldn't walk past, and we ignored them. ... I got into big trouble with the [gang] ... because some dude supposed to put a hit out on me or something. ... It seems like every summer they do that. ... They going to fight me and I'll be beating them up, and I don't play that ... [I have] to show them, like, man you all got the wrong one this time.

...

No, I just have to defend myself. I can't show them I'm no punk. Because if you show them you're a punk, they're going to try to take your lunch money. Yeah, it's like that ... like when I said they tried to put a hit on me last time, they supposed to try and kill me or something. Every time they see me, beat me up or something.

Girls talked about the particular threats they faced as young women living in chronically violent places.[21] One girl spoke of a close family member being raped, while another told us about her father being murdered. And, Briana, a former Dearborn resident who was 13 when we spoke to her in 2009, told us about coping with the all-too-common experience of threats of sexual assault and harassment:

> Ever since that boy told me he was going to rape me, I have a feeling that [I had less] protection, and [I had to keep] my protection built up. And like every time I walk to the stores, it be more men than women. So, I try to like, like, like—I try to like wear more baggy clothes than tight. And also my cousin who died 'cause somebody raped her. ... Or if I'm walking by myself I'll—I'll like have my fists balled up like this so no one touch me.

Perhaps it should not be so shocking that relocation and a modest improvement in housing quality and neighborhood safety did so little to change the trajectory for the children and youth we followed. The sad reality is that they had had already experienced more than their share of "adverse childhood events" and trauma just by virtue of spending their early years in the Wells and Dearborn Homes. Being forced to move is itself traumatic, and children did not receive the same level of support and counseling as their parents. In fact, since development plans often drove relocation schedules, kids often had to move in the middle of the school year. Once they moved, they often ended up in places that, while not as dangerous as their former public housing communities, still exposed them to violence and disorder. Finally, teenagers, especially young men, faced the threat of being targets in their new neighborhoods simply because they came from public housing communities dominated by rival gangs. Nothing in CHA's service package was aimed at addressing these very real threats to children's mental health and well-being and, in retrospect, it was likely unrealistic to think that relocation would be enough to overcome all of their other disadvantages, especially when so few of them moved to truly "good" neighborhoods.

HOST: REACHING THE NEXT GENERATION

Both my own team and my collaborators at the CHA, especially Mary Howard, were deeply disturbed by the disappointing findings about the outcomes for children and youth. As we prepared for the CHA's celebration of the 10th anniversary of the Plan in 2010, Mary and I began talking about trying to mount a second Demonstration that would attempt target services to children and youth to try to address the effects of trauma and living in communities mired in deep poverty. Our vision was a "two-generation" service model that would deliver high-quality services to the whole family instead of hoping that services that helped parents would automatically benefit their children.

The new project would focus on the largest of CHA's remaining traditional public housing developments, Altgeld Gardens, a profoundly isolated community located on the far south side of the city.[22] The development sits 25 miles south of Chicago's Loop, is served only by a single bus line, and is far from employment or other services. In 2005, the CHA completely renovated about 1,200 of the more than 1,900 units, updating the kitchens and bathrooms and replacing the heating and cooling systems. The CHA added laundry facilities, and a local group constructed a large community garden. The rest of the units are still vacant and boarded up, adding to the sense of isolation. There are five schools, a health clinic, and a Park District facility on or adjacent to the property, but the community has no grocery store or other amenities.

The area around Altgeld used to be home to numerous steel mills, industrial plants, and landfills. In the 1980s, the community was the focus of an environmental justice campaign; a young Barack Obama participated in the campaign as a community organizer. By 2010, most of CHA's high-rise developments had been demolished, and Altgeld was becoming a focus of attention of advocates

Photo 5.2 Altgeld Gardens, site of HOST Demonstration. Source: Photo by Susan Popkin.

from groups like BPI who were concerned about bringing resources to the community. But even so, we had no luck interesting local funders in supporting a new and ambitious demonstration and were becoming discouraged. Then in late October, I got an unexpected call from a representative from the Open Society Foundations (OSF) telling me the foundation was looking to support an effort to use housing as a platform to provide services as part of their "Special Poverty Alleviation Fund" initiative.[23] OSF had hoped to give the money directly to HUD to support its Choice Neighborhoods Initiative (the successor to the HOPE VI program), but at that point, Congress would not permit HUD to accept foundation funding. Staff in HUD's research office were familiar with the Demonstration and suggested that OSF give me a call to see if I had any ideas for a useful project. I told them about Mary's and my concept for a two-generation demonstration in Altgeld; the Foundation was interested, but asked me to design an even bigger project that would involve multiple housing authorities. With Mary, my team at the Urban Institute quickly laid the groundwork for what became the three-city HOST (Housing Opportunities and Services Together) Demonstration, which as of this writing, is still ongoing.[24]

HOST was an unusual project for the Urban Institute and for my team, requiring us to be much more intimately involved in developing a framework and theory of change for intervention we were planning to study, as well as conducting a "formative evaluation," meant to provide real-time ongoing feedback to our partners on the ground. This dual role meant we were much more intimately involved in managing and overseeing implementation than is typical for researchers—even more than we had been in the first Demonstration. In many ways, we were also acting as a funder; OSF had provided the funds that would support both services and research to us directly and helped connect me to other foundations to increase and sustain the services. The three participating housing authorities had to provide a funding match, but I spent what was for me an unprecedented amount of time and energy reaching out to funders and making sure that HOST remained high profile. OSF also wanted this project to have real policy impact, so my team and I spent a lot of time and energy on outreach and dissemination to policymakers and practitioners.

At the same time, we had to carry out a rigorous evaluation that met the standards of the Urban Institute—and ourselves. Although we did not follow the HOST families as intensively as we did the families in the Panel Study and the first Demonstration, we did conduct a baseline survey in 2011, as well as several rounds of focus groups and interviews with parents and teens. We also collected program data to monitor the sites' activities and conducted quarterly site visits, weekly and then biweekly phone calls with the site teams, and several rounds of interviews with site leadership and case managers. [25] Reflecting our intimate engagement with the sites and the local communities, we even held what we called "Data Walks" at all three sites to share our findings from our baseline survey and analysis of the program data. The Data Walks involved making posters with simple charts and bullet points, hanging them on the wall, and our staff literally walking around the room discussing the information on the charts with small groups of residents and service providers.[26]

Mary Howard provided a framework and general service model for HOST that the other sites could adapt to suit their communities and service providers. She also designed the specific service model for Altgeld, which drew on the previous Demonstration to define the "high-risk" families who would receive intensive case management with low caseloads (30-1), on-site clinical mental health services, and employment and training services for adults. In Altgeld, the program built on CHA's existing FamilyWorks case management services, which already reflected what we had learned from the first Demonstration. UCAN, a large nonprofit multiservice agency, was the existing FamilyWorks provider at Altgeld, and Mary and the CHA asked them to take on the challenge of providing the more intensive HOST services for adults and being part of the Urban Institute's evaluation. To provide similarly tailored support for children and youth, CHA contracted with Project Match, a venerable welfare-to-work program with a long history of working with CHA families. Finally, CHA used its administrative records to select 230 families to target for the intensive services who had not met the housing authority's work requirement—that every "work-able" resident age 18 or older be working, in school, or volunteering—for two consecutive quarters.

The HOST Demonstration ran in Altgeld from 2011 to 2014, serving as a rich laboratory for learning about the realities of implementing a two-generation approach to providing intensive services in a public housing setting. Among the many challenges was determining how to provide effective services for children and ensure they were successfully integrated with the services for adults. One factor that made serving children harder was the fact that there were simply so many of them—more than 450 in the 230 families. The apartments in Altgeld were large, and many families had several children ranging in age from infants and toddlers to teenagers. Another complication was that children's needs vary tremendously depending on their age, so one service model was unlikely to work for all. The HOST team in Chicago and in our other sites in Portland, Oregon, and Washington, DC, ended up primarily serving elementary and middle school-aged children—the largest group and the easiest to serve with group programs.

Coordinating the adult and youth teams proved more difficult than we or our service partners had anticipated. Getting to a point where the services were truly integrated required extensive relationship building, as well as work to develop shared data systems and indicators. UCAN leadership instituted a weekly family case conference to ensure that the different team members were working together effectively to serve the whole household. As in the first Demonstration, the intensive work was difficult and sometimes traumatic for the staff. Case managers had to learn to use techniques like motivational interviewing and strength-based counseling instead of the more typical program compliance model, i.e., ensuring residents were meeting the work requirement. This different type of approach meant investing in building with often-mistrustful residents and having to make repeated attempts at outreach and engagement instead of waiting for clients to come to the UCAN office. Because of the high level of need, UCAN leadership decided to provide additional training in trauma-informed care for their team. Finally, the demand for clinical mental health services for both adults and youth was high, and UCAN eventually had to bring in a second provider.[27]

The HOST experience has offered and continues to offer important lessons about the need for better solutions to address the challenges that face the deeply poor children who live in public housing. Public housing developments in Chicago and other cities may generally be better managed and safer than they were in the 1990s, but they still comprise some of the poorest communities in the nation and so suffer from all the ails of concentrated poverty and chronic disadvantage that can threaten children's well-being. The experience of being intimately involved in developing and implementing HOST highlighted some of the obvious and not-so-obvious ways that living in these communities affected children's health and development. Among the more obvious were the parents with mental health challenges. I interviewed one woman who told me she was so depressed that she had not gotten out of bed for months and refused to open her door to her HOST case manager until her son got involved in a support group UCAN was running for teen boys; he brought the case manager and clinician to their house. The clinician convinced her to see a psychiatrist, who diagnosed her bipolar disorder and got her on medication; with her feeling better, her son was finally able to focus on school. HOST families were also dealing with an array of other complex problems, including domestic violence, substance abuse, serious physical health problems, unstable employment, and incarcerated family members—all of which had the potential to create chaotic and traumatic situations for their children.[28]

Chronic community violence was another obvious problem: even though Altgeld had security patrols, it was so large and had so many winding streets and cul-de-sacs that it was extremely difficult to secure. The vacant buildings were an easy target for squatters and drug dealers. Members of a rival gang from neighboring development had no trouble getting on the property and clashing with Altgeld youth. We visited the development on a day when the shooting was so bad that residents could not go outside—apparently a not-uncommon situation. A woman I interviewed that morning told me she was so anxious and stressed about her children's safety that she was unable to sleep; she relied on her HOST case manager to make sure that they were enrolled in after-school programs and activities to keep them off the streets. I am sure that her children found the situation just as stressful and traumatic.

And then there were the less obvious problems: at our baseline survey, residents from all three of our HOST sites reported high levels of food insecurity.[29] In Altgeld, about half the residents told us that they had problems affording enough food, a rate more than twice the national average of 20 percent. The high rates of food insecurity surprised us; after all, HOST families had housing subsidies and other benefits and, in theory, should have been better off than other poor families. But two years into the project, we were stunned to learn through our work in our DC HOST site that the problem was so severe residents reported that some local girls were resorting to trading sexual favors for food. We were able to partner with Feeding America, the national network of food banks, and conduct targeted focus groups with teen boys and girls in all three of our HOST sites. In all three places, we heard the same sad stories—kids who were desperately hungry and ashamed, who went hungry so their younger siblings could eat, who sometimes stole

Photo 5.3 Children at food giveaway in Cabrini-Green. Source: Photo by Kyle Higgins.

or dealt drugs to earn money, and yes, sometimes traded sex for food or money. Altgeld teens were intimately familiar with these problems and made eloquent and poignant comments about how "normal" it was to not have enough food in their community. When we expanded the study to include teens who lived outside of public housing, we found that these problems were widespread, but that they appeared to be most severe in these deeply poor communities.[30]

Finally, HOST also highlighted the need to find creative solutions for the youngest children—the zero- to five-year-olds who would not directly benefit from case management or clinical services, but who were the most vulnerable to trauma and developmental delays. Altgeld actually had two Head Start programs on site, but families were often reluctant to trust their children to their care or used the programs more as a drop-in day care than for real early childhood education. BPI started a small home-visiting program to bring parenting training and support to young mothers, but it was intended only for first-time parents who were 21 years old or younger. Many young children live in households with older parents and multiple siblings, and their parents also need services and support to help them get off to a good start. As of this writing, we are collaborating again with Mary Howard and her team to develop and test a model for families with very young children that combines high-quality home visiting with clinical mental health services.[31]

Finally, in addition to shedding light on some of the factors that put public housing children at such high risk and suggesting some new approaches, HOST has provided important lessons for what it takes to use housing as a platform for intensive, high-quality services.[32] Housing authorities are essentially landlords and property managers; they are not used to providing social services, and HUD does not really provide them with funding to do so in a meaningful way. The HOST sites are all MTW agencies; that means they have more flexibility in how to use their funds. But as I've said repeatedly throughout this chapter, housing authorities house some of the poorest and most vulnerable children in the United States. Our work with the first three HOST sites has shown that helping these agencies to collaborate with service providers to make high-quality services accessible to their families has the potential to pay off in better outcomes for both adults and children—and, in doing so, to make public housing developments stronger, healthier communities overall.

Numerous other housing authorities and affordable housing developers continue to approach me to learn how they can bring services like HOST to their residents. The need is clear, as is the desire to improve the life chances for these very vulnerable children and youth. As I have stated elsewhere in this book, the fact that CHA now has one of the most innovative and well-funded housing authority Resident Services Department in the nation is one of the most surprising results of the Plan. My collaboration with Mary Howard has already led to innovations in using housing as a platform for service delivery that offer important lessons for practitioners and policymakers and that gives me hope that at least some of CHA's children may have better lives as a result. But, as I will discuss in the final chapter, unless we address some of the bigger structural problems that continue to trap too many very low-income families of color in poor, crime-ridden communities, even the most innovative, state-of-the-art two-generation programs can offer little more than a Band Aid.

NOTES

1. See Megan Sandel, MD. 2014. "Can the Housing Vaccine Help a Community? Thinking from People to Populations." Children's Health Watch, Posted November 4, 2014. http://www.childrenshealthwatch.org/2014/11/can-housing-vaccine-help-community-thinking-people-populations/.

2. Susan J. Popkin and Liza Getsinger. 2010. Reaching the Next Generation: The Crisis for CHA's Youth. Supporting Vulnerable Public Housing Families, Brief No. 6. Washington, DC: The Urban Institute. http://www.urban.org/research/publication/reaching-next-generation-crisis-chas-youth; Megan Gallagher. 2010. CHA Transformation: Children and Youth. CHA Families and the Plan for Transformation, Brief No. 4. Washington, DC: The Urban Institute. http://www.urban.org/research/publication/cha-transformation-children-and-youth; Chantal Hailey and Megan Gallagher. 2013. Chronic Violence: Beyond the Developments. Long-Term Outcomes for CHA Families, Brief No. 5. Washington, DC: The Urban Institute. http://www.urban.org/research/publication/chronic-violence-beyond-developments.

3. See also Thomas D. Boston. 2009. "Public Housing Transformation and Family Self-Sufficiency: A Case Study of Chicago and Atlanta Housing Authorities," (draft) and Brian A. Jacob 2004. "Public Housing Vouchers, and Student Achievement: Evidence from Public Housing Demolitions in Chicago," *American Economic Review* 94(1) (Mar): 233–258.

4. Raj Chetty's recent research on the Moving to Opportunity Demonstration found evidence of long-term positive effects on earnings for children whose families moved from public housing to low-poverty communities; however, few CHA children ended up in "opportunity" neighborhoods and are not likely to fare as well. See Raj Chetty, Nathaniel Hendren, and Lawrence Katz. 2015. The Effects of Exposure to Better Neighborhoods on Children: New Evidence from the Moving to Opportunity Experiment. National Bureau of Economic Research Working Paper. http://www.equality-of-opportunity.org/images/mto_paper.pdf.

5. See Hailey and Gallagher. 2013, note 2. and Susan J. Popkin, Megan Gallagher, Elizabeth Davies, Larry Buron, and Christopher R. Hayes. 2013. CHA Families and the Plan for Transformation. Long-Term Outcomes for CHA Families, Brief No. 2. Washington, DC: The Urban Institute. http://www.urban.org/research/publication/cha-residents-and-plan-transformation.

6. It was not always possible to get information about the same child because some children moved out of the household during the course of the study.

7. Much of the material in this section is adapted from Hailey and Gallagher. 2013, see note 2.

8. Robert Sampson. 2012. *Great American City: Chicago and the Enduring Neighborhood Effect.* Chicago: University of Chicago Press.

9. For information on the baseline of the HOPE VI Panel Study, see Susan J. Popkin, Diane K. Levy, Laura E. Harris, Jennifer Comey, Mary K. Cunningham, and Larry F. Buron. 2002. HOPE VI Panel Study: Baseline Report. Washington, DC: The Urban Institute. http://www.urban.org/research/publication/hope-vi-panel-study-baseline-report. For information on the baseline for the Chicago Family Case Management Demonstration, see Susan J. Popkin, Brett Theodos, Caterina Roman, and Elizabeth Guernsey. 2008. The Chicago Family Case Management Demonstration: Developing a New Model for Serving "Hard to House" Public Housing Families. Washington, DC: Urban Institute. http://www.urban.org/publications/411708.html.

10. Larry Buron, Christopher R. Hayes, and Chantal Hailey. 2013. An Improved Living Environment, but … Long-Term Outcomes for CHA Residents, Brief No. 3. Washington, DC: The Urban Institute. http://www.urban.org/research/publication/improved-living-environment.

11. James Garbarino, Kathleen Kostelny, and Nancy Dubrow. 1991. *No Place to Be a Child: Growing Up in a War Zone.* New York: Lexington Books; Susan J. Popkin, Tama Leventhal, and Gretchen Weissman. 2010. "Girls in the 'Hood: How Safety Affects the Life Chances of Low-Income Girls." *Urban Affairs Review* 45(6): 715–774.

12. Hooven, Carole, Paula Nurius, Patricia LoganGreene, and Elaine Thompson. 2012. "Childhood Violence Exposure: Cumulative and Specific Effects on Adult Mental Health." *Journal of Family Violence* 27(6): 511–522. Also see research from the ACES study, e.g., Vanessa Sacks, David Murphey, and Kristen Moore. 2014. Adverse Childhood Experiences: National and State-Level Prevalence. Research Brief 2014-28. Washington, DC: ChildTrends. http://www.childtrends.org/wp-content/uploads/2014/07/Brief-adverse-childhood-experiences_FINAL.pdf.

13. Popkin et al. 2000. *The Hidden War*; Turner, Popkin, and Rawlings. 2009. *Public Housing and the Legacy of Segregation*; Susan J. Popkin and Marla McDaniel. 2013. HOST: Can Public Housing be a Platform for Change. HOST Working Paper. Washington, DC: The Urban Institute. http://www.urban.org/UploadedPDF/412965-host-can-public-housing.pdf.

14. Respondents were asked if over the previous year their children had been involved in any of the following nine activities: being suspended or expelled from school, going to a juvenile court, having a problem with alcohol or drugs, getting into trouble with the police, doing something illegal for money, getting pregnant or getting someone else pregnant, being in a gang, being arrested, and being in jail or incarcerated. We measured the proportion of children involved in two or more of these behaviors.

15. Developed in 1996 by Jim Connell and Lisa J. Bridges at the Institute for Research and Reform in Education in California, this measure attempts to assess the level of child's interest and willingness to do their schoolwork. Each head of

household was asked four questions about whether the child cares about doing well in school, only works on homework when forced to, does just enough homework to get by, or always does his or her homework. The answers were scored on a scale from 1 to 4, where 1 means none of the time and 4 means all the time (answers to the negative items were scored in reverse). We measured the proportion of children with a high level of school engagement, which is equivalent to a scale score of 15 or more.

16. Peter Edelman, Harry Holzer, and Paul Offner. 2006. *Reconnecting Disadvantaged Young Men*. Washington, DC: Urban Institute Press.

17. Susan J. Popkin, Megan Gallagher, Elizabeth Davies, Larry Buron, and Christopher R. Hayes. 2013. CHA Families and the Plan for Transformation. Long-Term Outcomes for CHA Families, Brief No. 2. Washington, DC: The Urban Institute. http://www.urban.org/research/publication/cha-residents-and-plan-transformation.

18. Briggs, Popkin, and Goering. 2010. *Moving to Opportunity*; Scanlon, Edward, and Kevin Devine. 2001. "Residential Mobility and Youth Well-Being: Research, Policy, and Practice Issues." *Journal of Sociology and Social Welfare* 28(1): 119–138.

19. We heard the same issues in our interviews with families who relocated as part of the Moving to Opportunity Demonstration. See Briggs, Popkin, and Goering. 2010.

20. Christopher Hayes, Graham McDonald, Susan J. Popkin, Leah Hendey, and Allison Stolte. 2013. "Public Housing Transformation and Crime: Are Relocatees More Likely to Be Offenders or Victims?" *Cityscape* 15(3): 9–35. https://www.huduser.gov/portal/periodicals/cityscpe/vol15num3/article1.html.

21. For a discussion of the issue of coercive sexual environments and their impact on girls and women's mental health and well-being, see Susan. J. Popkin, Chantal Hailey, Janine Zweig, Nan Astone, Reed Jordan, Leah Gordon, and Jay Silverman. 2016. "Coercive Sexual Environments: Exploring the Linkages to Mental Health in Public Housing." *Cityscape* 18(1): 165–182.

22. Chantal Hailey and Priya Saxena. 2013. HOST: Helping Families, Building Community. HOST, Brief No. 5. Washington, DC: The Urban Institute. http://www.urban.org/sites/default/files/alfresco/publication-pdfs/412952-HOST-Helping-Families-Building-Communities.pdf.

23. Susan J. Popkin, Molly M. Scott, Joe Parilla, Elsa Falkenburger, and Shinwon Kyung. 2012. Planning the Housing Opportunities and Services Together Demonstration. HOST Brief No. 1. Washington, DC: The Urban Institute. http://www.urban.org/research/publication/planning-housing-opportunity-and-services-together-demonstration.

24. Susan J. Popkin and Marla McDaniel. 2013. Can Public Housing Be a Platform for Change? Washington, DC: The Urban Institute. http://www.urban.org/research/publication/host-can-public-housing-be-platform-change.

25. See Susan J. Popkin, Molly M. Scott, Joe Parilla, Elsa Falkenburger, and Shinwon Kyung. 2012. Planning the Housing Opportunities and Services Together Demonstration. HOST Brief No. 1. Washington, DC: The Urban Institute. http://www.urban.org/research/publication/planning-housing-opportunity-and-services-together-demonstration; Susan J. Popkin and Marla McDaniel. 2013. Can Public Housing Be a Platform for Change? Washington, DC: The Urban Institute. http://www.urban.org/research/publication/host-can-public-housing-be-platform-change.

26. See Brittany Murray, Elsa Falkenburger, and Priya Saxena. 2015. Data Walks: An Innovative Way to Share Data with Communities. Washington, DC: The Urban Institute. http://www.urban.org/research/publication/data-walks-innovative-way-share-data-communities.

27. For more detail on the HOST Demonstration, see Molly M. Scott, Susan J. Popkin, and Priya Saxena. 2016. Making a Two-Generation Approach Work in the Real World: Lessons from the HOST Demonstration. Washington, DC: The Urban Institute. http://www.urban.org/research/publication/making-two-generation-model-work-real-world.

28. See Molly M. Scott, Susan J. Popkin, Marla McDaniel, Priya Saxena, and Reed Jordan. 2013. Serving HOST Families: The Challenges to Overcome. Housing Opportunities and Services Together, Brief No. 3. Washington, DC: The Urban Institute. http://www.urban.org/research/publication/serving-host-families-challenges-overcome.

29. See Molly M. Scott, Susan J. Popkin, Marla McDaniel, Priya Saxena, and Reed Jordan. 2013. Serving HOST Families: The Challenges to Overcome. Housing Opportunities and Services Together, Brief No. 3. Washington, DC: The Urban Institute. http://www.urban.org/research/publication/serving-host-families-challenges-overcome.

30. This work will be released in a new Urban Institute report in September 2016.

31. See Marla McDaniel, S. Darius Tandon, Caroline Heller, Gina Adams, and Susan J. Popkin. 2015. Addressing Parents' Mental Health Needs in Home Visiting Services in Public Housing. Washington, DC: The Urban Institute. http://www.urban.org/research/publication/addressing-parents-mental-health-home-visiting-services-public-housing.

32. See Sarah Gillespie and Susan J. Popkin. 2015. Building Housing Authority Capacity for Better Resident Services. Washington, DC: The Urban Institute. http://www.urban.org/research/publication/building-public-housing-authority-capacity-better-resident-services.

Chapter Six

No Simple Solutions

It has now been more than 15 years since the CHA launched the Plan for Transformation, and people frequently ask me what I think about the changes. Generally, they want me to confirm their belief that it has been a failure—it is a sad reflection on CHA's long-standing reputation that almost no one ever asks me whether it was a success. At the CHA's 10 year anniversary celebration, I said that I had started out very skeptical and had publicly predicted that it was likely that the Plan would be just one more blow for long-suffering residents. I was happily surprised that things had turned out better than I had ever imagined. As I stated in the introduction, the CHA and its partners were ill prepared to handle the demands of the ambitious plans, especially the complex financing deals and overseeing and coordinating the redevelopment. The agency was even less prepared for the enormous challenges that would come with needing to relocate tens of thousands of very poor, very vulnerable residents, many of whom had never lived anywhere else.

But, as I've said repeatedly throughout this book, the reality was both better and more complex than I could have predicted. The best thing is that there is now no public housing left in Chicago that is as bad—as dangerous, as poor quality—as the developments that came down. The children growing up in CHA housing—or whose families have vouchers—are living in better housing in safer neighborhoods than the children whose families lived through the CHA's worst days. The residents we followed over 10 years told us about the relief that came with enjoying things most of us take for granted: sleeping through the night without fear; letting their children play outside; and expecting the heat to work when it was cold outside. These changes meant less worry and anxiety for many of the people we followed, an important mental health benefit that could have longer-term pay offs for them and for their children. But it is also true that only a small proportion—less than

20 percent of the families we followed—ended up in the new mixed-income developments and that even fewer ended up in low-poverty "opportunity" neighborhoods that offered a truly different quality of life. Most of the residents in our studies used vouchers to move to other poor, minority neighborhoods like Englewood on the city's west side or South Shore on the southeast. The rest ended up in—and were mostly satisfied with—apartments in newly refurbished public housing developments. The experience of the Chicago Family Case Management Demonstration showed that it was possible to use wrap-around services to improve residents' lives in important ways—and for the CHA to build a strong resident services program. But even though many hard to house residents reported successful relocation, high rates of employment, and better mental and physical health at the end of three years, there is no question that even those who gained the most still struggled with multiple challenges. And the biggest disappointment is that the Plan, which, after all, really did rescue thousands of children from the most dangerous places in Chicago, seemed to have little impact on their overall well-being. The HOST Demonstration work has created a laboratory for testing approaches to try to better serve CHA's children, but we are a long way from being able to take these efforts to scale. As I discuss below, the sad reality is that solving those deep problems and ensuring those children a brighter future will require a much more substantial and longer-term commitment.

The Plan also had a profound effect on the CHA itself. It is important to remember that through the 1980s and 1990s—up until the HUD takeover in 1995—the CHA was the most dysfunctional housing authority in the country. Its high-rise developments were notorious, dangerous, and dilapidated buildings overrun with gang activity and drug dealing. Our analysis for the CHA crime project showed that in 1999, the CHA's properties were the most dangerous places in Chicago; tearing down the projects brought an almost immediate and long-lasting citywide reduction in violent crime.[1] In fact, the obvious reason that the residents we followed consistently reported feeling so much safer is that there was literally *nowhere* they could have moved that would have been as dangerous as CHA's developments. And one of the reasons the CHA was so dysfunctional for so long was that the agency had spent decades battling a losing war on violent crime, leaving it with few resources to carry out its basic functions as a landlord and property manager.[2]

The experience of implementing the Plan changed the agency profoundly. It had to develop the capacity to carry out complex real estate deals, implement equally complex redevelopment plans, and deliver high-quality relocation and resident services. In the early years of the Plan, the agency struggled to deliver in all of these areas: financing deals stalled (or collapsed, as was the case for the first plan for Wells); redevelopment plans languished and residents were stranded for years in half-empty buildings; and the relocation and resident services were so bad that a coalition of advocacy groups filed suit. But by 2010, redevelopment was well underway across the city, and CHA had a resident services program that was the envy of other housing authorities. There is no question that a major factor underlying this success was the fact that Mayor Daley and the MacArthur Foundation committed their power and resources to making the CHA's transformation a true civic enterprise. Daley appointed his close ally, Terry Peterson, to head agency during the critical early phases of the transformation and used his clout in Washington, Springfield, and Chicago to make sure that CHA had the funds it needed for its ambitious plans. Julia Stasch, his former housing director, went to MacArthur; she and Jonathan Fanton, the then-president, made an unprecedented commitment of funds and staff resources to support the Plan and to bring other philanthropy to the table. And over the years, MacArthur provided generous support for researchers (including me), advocates, and journalists to monitor and document the CHA's progress. All of this monitoring had the effect of holding the CHA and the City accountable for delivering on their promises and avoiding some of the egregious mistakes that occurred in other cities like "losing" the displaced residents and not providing replacement housing.

So, for all of these reasons, in 2010, at the CHA's event and in articles I wrote, I said that the Plan for Transformation had been much more of a success than I would have ever predicted.[3] But the view from January 2016 is less rosy. Daley's successor, Mayor Rahm Emanuel, has not shown the same level of commitment to the CHA and the Plan, and his decisions have undermined the agency in many ways. He made clear early on that the Plan was Daley's priority, not his, and that his administration was going to instead focus on fixing Chicago's schools—an effort that thus far has led to multiple teacher strikes and little progress. And just months after his election, he made what was in my and many other observers' views a remarkably poor decision to fire then-CHA CEO Lewis Jordan over a minor scandal involving use of his agency credit card.[4] Jordan had been CEO for six years and had been at the helm as the CHA transitioned from the struggles of the early years of implementation to the successful position it achieved by 2010.

Emanuel replaced Jordan with Charles Woodyard from the much-smaller Charlotte Housing Authority, and put his own management team in place; Woodyard resigned two years later in the wake of a sexual harassment scandal.[5] His departure set off a revolving door, with the result that the CHA has now had five CEOs in as many years, a very tough scenario for any organization. The latest, Eugene Jones, seems poised to bring some stability back to the agency, but the turmoil of the past five years has caused real and serious problems and undermined morale. The Plan has all but stalled, progress on the mixed-income housing has slowed to a crawl, and the agency is facing major pressures from advocates over the lack of progress in the face of a growing affordable housing crisis. Another area of conflict is whether the CHA should move forward with plans to replace the Lathrop Homes and Cabrini Rowhouses with mixed-income housing, or should simply rehab these developments and leave them so that poor families have a chance to live in affluent communities. As of this writing, new plans have been approved, and Jones is now poised to move forward with redevelopment at both sites. Another challenge he faces is making a final determination on whether to rehab or demolish the vacant buildings in Altgeld Gardens, the HOST Demonstration site. Some advocates are pushing for reopening all of the vacant units to provide housing for the homeless, while others oppose it because that would mean even more families living in extreme poverty and isolation. At the same time, the agency must determine how it will maintain the funding that allows it to provide high-quality resident services and manage what is now an enormous voucher program serving more than 40,000 households. Again, the signs from CHA's new leadership are encouraging—Jones is supporting a HOST spin-off that will test a home-visiting model for families with very young children. But dealing with all of these challenges will require strong and effective leadership both within the CHA and from City Hall.

Another challenge facing the CHA is that the MacArthur Foundation has gone through its own transitions and is no longer investing as heavily in supporting the CHA. Julia Stasch became President of the Foundation in 2015, and while it still supports work intended to benefit Chicago, the Foundation has a new set of priorities, including a focus on ending nuclear proliferation and juvenile justice. The Partnership for New Communities dissolved in 2012, ending another important source of support for the CHA's services and workforce efforts.[6] The net result of the changes in city government and at MacArthur is that the CHA has less civic support than it did 15 years ago, so it will be more difficult for the agency to find allies or funding partners for the kinds of innovative special projects and initiatives that have made it stand out as a leader in the field.

Finally, CHA, like all housing authorities, continues to face serious threats at the federal level. Since 2000, Congress has consistently cut funds for public housing and vouchers, leaving housing authorities struggling to keep up with the demands of management and maintenance of an aging housing stock—media accounts claim that the outstanding capital costs for the New York City Housing Authority, the largest in the nation, exceed *$18 billion*.[7] At the same time, the demand for affordable housing continues to grow. Since unlike other federal safety net programs, housing assistance is not an entitlement, nationally only one in four eligible households is lucky enough to receive a subsidy.[8] Like most housing authorities, the CHA maintains an enormous waiting list; more than 80,000 people signed up the last

Photo 6.1 Playground in Cabrini-Green. Source: Photo by Kyle Higgins.

time the agency opened up its list in 2014. CHA remains a MTW agency, which gives it flexibility in how it allocates its federal funds. But with the housing shortage, the pressure to allocate those funds exclusively to housing units or vouchers instead of resident services and management will continue to grow. As of this writing, the CHA still has a large and controversial funding reserve, which is supposed to support the remaining redevelopment work; when those funds are expended, the agency will have less flexibility to support the kinds of innovation that led to the Case Management Demonstration and HOST.[9]

NO SIMPLE SOLUTIONS ...

My main purpose in writing this book—and doing this work—has been to call attention to the plight of the thousands of families who endured the worst days of public housing and now have had to navigate the changes wrought by the Plan for Transformation. I have ended virtually every article, book, report, and speech I have written over the past 15 years by stressing that there are no

simple solutions to the deep challenges facing CHA families and none that
are inexpensive. Addressing the deep needs of families scarred by generations
of living with the stress and traumatizing effects of deep poverty and chronic
violence will require significant, large-scale, and sustained investments that
address the problems of poor neighborhoods, ensure residents the choice to
move to places that offer them the chance for better opportunities for themselves and their children, and provide the kinds of services and supports that
can address the trauma that is the legacy of segregation and discrimination.[10]

It is not clear to me that we, as a nation, have the political will to make these
kinds of commitments and to address the structural challenges of growing
inequality and worsening racial segregation that continue to undermine the
life chances of too many children of color trapped in distressed communities.
But Chicago's experience offers important lessons for national policy, and
CHA's children, like other children growing up in deeply poor communities,
cannot afford to wait. And surely we cannot afford to lose another generation
to the violence, bad schools, and, frankly, our own indifference. It distresses
me that so many view public housing children as somehow undeserving or at
fault for their own problems. Focus groups we conducted for our study of the
effects of the Plan on crime made clear that even residents from Chicago's
other poor African-American communities hold extremely negative views of
people who come from "the projects."[11] The number of phone calls I continue
to get from reporters asking me to comment on whether public housing relocatees are responsible for any and all crime in their cities continues to astound
and sadden me. But even in the face of all of these challenges, I believe we
must do what we can to help our most vulnerable children.

My first set of recommendations focus on Chicago and not losing the
ground the CHA has gained. The political and consequent management turmoil of last five years should be raising alarms about the sustainability of the
management improvements at the CHA and the agency's ability to remain
effective in carrying out the Plan's ambitious goals. The fact that Gene Jones
has now been officially appointed to be the CEO is an encouraging sign
and, hopefully, he will be able to bring stability to the agency. Federal and
local policymakers must ensure that he and the CHA have the support they
need to carry out this work and that the agency uses the best approaches to
implementing what my colleague Margery Turner calls "place conscious"
strategies.[12] The City and HUD must maintain the political and financial
investment in Chicago's public housing transformation—and advocates must
keep up the pressure to make them do so—in order to make sure that CHA's
management stays strong and that the agency is able to deliver on its promises
to its families and communities. That means that CHA leadership is able to
ensure that the deals for the final mixed-income developments go through, the
construction is completed on a timely basis, and there is strong oversight to

ensure that these new communities remain decent, safe, and attractive places for both low- and higher-income households. It also means keeping up the momentum for investment in and around the new developments to ensure that they become attractive places to live, that residents have access to shopping and other amenities, and that kids have decent schools to attend.

The second recommendation is that CHA should build on Chicago's long history of promoting mobility for public housing families to offer a new, state-of-the art and well-funded mobility program for its residents. New research on the children whose families who moved to lower-poverty communities through the Gautreaux program and the Moving to Opportunity Demonstration shows long-term gains in education and income.[13] Thus far, even though the CHA's partners have offered residents mobility counseling services, the evidence shows that CHA's Plan for Transformation has done little to promote moves to neighborhoods that offer a meaningful difference in the types of opportunities they offer. We know from the experience of the Chicago Family Case Management Demonstration that one reason so few have made these moves is that the families still living in CHA housing when the Plan began were, for the most part, extremely vulnerable and dealing with multiple complex problems. Being forced to move from their long-time homes, bad as they were, was traumatic enough; they were simply not prepared to take on the additional demands of moving to completely unfamiliar areas. But 15 years into the Plan, some of these families have been living in the private market with their vouchers for years. Our research makes clear that many are dissatisfied with conditions in the kinds of communities that are easily accessible with their vouchers. These dissatisfied voucher holders might be now more ready to consider a more radical type of move to a different type of community. The CHA made some attempts to implement a second-mover program early on in the Plan; the program had only modest success. There is interest at the federal level; the Obama administration proposed new funds for a national housing mobility initiative in its FY2017 budget. I believe the idea of promoting mobility for successful voucher holders is worth revisiting, especially in light of the compelling findings about the long-term benefits for the MTO children.[14]

Third, we as a society need to make a serious investment in targeted services and supports for "high-risk" public housing families in Chicago and elsewhere. As I've stated repeatedly throughout this book, public housing serves a large number of deeply poor families; the fact that these families are clustered in small geographic areas means that this housing makes an ideal—and efficient—platform for reaching some of the highest-need children in the nation. But too often, HUD and housing authorities are not at the table when policymakers are debating how to allocate service resources. The CHA currently has a well-funded and well-run Resident

Photo 6.2 Girls in Cabrini. Source: Photo by Kyle Higgins.

Services Department, and its FamilyWorks program provides case management at all of its public and mixed-income sites. But the reality is that even
this well-funded program is only able to support a modest level of service;
the CHA is large, and its programs have to serve its many senior buildings
and its family properties. It was only with the kind of external resources I was
able to bring through HOST that CHA could fund a provider to experiment
with low caseloads and the kinds of wrap-around services that might have
a longer-term impact on children and youth. And, like too many good programs, the funding was short-term, meaning that the intensive services were
not sustainable. Federal, state, and city funding streams rarely allow for the
kind of long-term relationship building and whole-family supports that can
help even the most vulnerable families to achieve stability and start to address
some of their deep challenges.

There is nothing magical about HOST or other high-quality two-generation
service models; they represent what we know about the best ways to provide social services to achieve the best results for families. We have seen
these approaches work in models like transitional and permanent supportive
housing for homeless families—people who grapple with the same kinds

of problems as those living in distressed public housing. The argument against making these types of services more widely available is inevitably that, even with careful targeting, they cost too much and that we cannot prove the "return on investment." I would argue that we cannot afford *not* to make these investments in families with children. If we don't help them now, we will pay through costs for medical care, emergency room visits, and incarceration—and, since this book is about public housing, in costs for property management and repairs. Finally, there is the fact that we are talking about the children we as a society need to sustain our economy, fill the jobs the baby boomers will leave as they retire, and fill the demand for caregivers for our growing number of frail elders.

Fourth, with its innovative Resident Services leadership, the CHA has the opportunity to be a laboratory for solving another pressing problem: how to bring services to the millions of families using vouchers to rent in the private market. There are more families in Chicago—and across the nation—who receive vouchers than live in public housing. Developing the kinds of close relationships and high levels of engagement that a high-quality program model like HOST delivers requires service providers to make regular home visits, which is much more difficult when you consider that voucher holders live all over, not clustered in one relatively small geographic area. Because the Chicago Family Case Management Demonstration involved relocation, we did experiment with serving voucher holders, and the providers were generally able to sustain contact. But stories like that of Annette and her children show that being out in the private market and far from service providers' offices meant that it was difficult to really head off crises. Serving families with vouchers effectively—and at scale—will require a significant investment of resources and new approaches such as creating "service hubs" where residents can drop in to see case managers and receive services. And ensuring that programs serve children and youth effectively will require even more creativity: we know that home-visiting models work for very young children, and those services are currently funded via the Affordable Care Act. But we know much less about how to reach older children and youth and ensure that they get the kind of sustained and teen-friendly attention that can help them to do well in school and have successful transitions to adulthood.

Fifth, as my colleagues Kathryn Edin and Luke Shaefer argue in their powerful book, *$2 A Day: Living on Almost Nothing in America*, we need to repair our nation's fraying safety net.[15] As Edin and Shaefer state, poor people want to work and most of them cycle in and out of low-wage jobs rather than depend on public assistance. That was certainly the case for the public housing residents we followed through the various studies I have described in this book—most of them worked at least some of the time. We need to make the fixes to our welfare programs that will support making work pay, and we need to ensure that housing assistance programs help support that goal. That means that federal and local policymakers need to experiment with strategies that do not penalize public and assisted housing residents for working by raising their rent for every dollar they earn. They also need to address the problem of the steep "cliffs" that occur when residents earn enough to no longer qualify for assistance.[16] Further, if we want to reduce the stigma associated with living in public housing and help residents stay connected to the labor market, then we need to continue to invest in strategies like Chicago's Transitional Jobs program. The program was a serious effort to address some of the barriers that keep public housing residents out of the labor market and to help offer participants a chance to work right away rather than languish in training programs. Our findings from the Chicago Family Case Management Demonstration showed how successful this approach was in getting even very troubled people back into the labor force.

Finally, building on the last point, we must address the flaws in our safety net that leave children so desperate and food insecure that that they are faced with impossible choices, from going without food to stealing, selling drugs, and even trading sex for money, food, and other basic necessities. The fact that our research has found this happening in even public housing where, presumably, having a housing subsidy should be at least somewhat protective is shocking. In the short term, we need teen-friendly food assistance programs, but in the long-run, Congress needs to address the flaws in SNAP, Temporary Assistance for Needy Families (TANF), and our workforce support programs that leave our poorest children so terribly vulnerable. We also desperately need solutions to the chronic violence that plagues our poorest, most racially-segregated communities. Until we address these terrible problems, we can expect that the children who live in CHA and other high-poverty public housing communities will fare little better—and perhaps even worse—than their parents.

NOTES

1. Susan J. Popkin, Michael J. Rich, Chris Hayes, Leah Hendey, and Joe Parilla. 2012. "Public Housing Transformation and Crime: Making the Case for Responsible Relocation." *Cityscape* 14(3): 137–160 http://www.huduser.gov/portal/periodicals/cityscpe/vol14num3/Cityscape_Nov2012_pub_house_trans.pdf.

2. Susan J. Popkin, Victoria E. Gwiasda, Dennis P. Rosenbaum, Lynn M. Olson, and Larry Buron. 2000. *The Hidden War: Crime and the Tragedy of Public Housing in Chicago.* New Brunswick, NJ: Rutgers University Press.

3. See Susan J. Popkin. 2010. "A Glass Half-Empty: Public Housing Families in Transition." *Housing Policy Debate* 20(1): 42–62; Susan J. Popkin, Megan Gallagher, Chantal Hailey, Elizabeth Davies, Larry Buron, and Christopher Hayes. 2013. CHA Residents and the Plan for Transformation. Long-Term Outcomes for CHA Residents,

Brief No. 2. Washington, DC: The Urban Institute. http://www.urban.org/publications/412761.html.

4. http://articles.chicagotribune.com/2011-06-14/news/chi-clout-street-embattled-cha-ceo-lewis-jordan-resigns-20110614_1_credit-card-jordans-public-housing.

5. http://www.wbez.org/news/former-cha-ceo-woodyard-resigned-amid-sexual-harassment-allegations-109182.

6. https://www.macfound.org/media/article_pdfs/ASSESSMENT_REPORT_OCT2011_FINAL.pdf.

7. http://www.nytimes.com/2014/08/12/nyregion/new-york-public-housing-faces-crisis-as-demands-and-deficits-grow.html.

8. Joint Center on Housing Studies Harvard University. 2015. *America's Rental Housing—Evolving Markets and Needs.* Boston: Harvard University. http://www.jchs.harvard.edu/sites/jchs.harvard.edu/files/ahr2013_01-intro.pdf.

9. https://www.dnainfo.com/chicago/20150708/bronzeville/hud-secretary-says-cha-sitting-on-too-much-money.

10. See Turner, Margery A., Susan J. Popkin, and Lynette Rawlings. 2009. *Public Housing Transformation: The Legacy of Segregation.* Washington DC: The Urban Institute Press.

11. See Susan J. Popkin, Michael J. Rich, Leah Hendey, Chris Hayes, Joseph Parilla, and George Galster. 2012. "Public Housing Transformation and Crime: Making the Case For Responsible Relocation." *Cityscape.* 14(3): 137–160. http://www.huduser.org/portal/periodicals/cityscpe/vol14num3/Cityscape_Nov2012_pub_house_trans.pdf.

12. Margery A. Turner, Peter Edelman, Erika Poethig, and Laudan Aron. 2014. *Tackling Persistent Poverty in Distressed Urban Neighborhoods.* Washington, DC: The Urban Institute. http://www.urban.org/research/publication/tackling-persistent-poverty-distressed-urban-neighborhoods.

13. See Raj Chetty, Nathaniel Hendren, and Lawrence Katz. 2015. The Effects of Exposure to Better Neighborhoods on Children: New Evidence from the Moving to Opportunity Experiment. National Bureau of Economic Research Working Paper. http://www.equality-of-opportunity.org/images/mto_paper.pdf.

14. Mary K. Cunningham, Susan J. Popkin, Erin B. Godfrey, Beata A. Bednarz, Janet L. Smith, Anne Knepler, and Doug Schenkelberg. 2001. *CHAC Mobility Program: Interim Assessment.* Washington, DC: The Urban Institute. http://www.urban.org/research/publication/chac-mobility-program-assessment.

15. Kathryn J. Edin and H. Luke Shaefer. 2015. *$2 A Day: Living on Almost Nothing in America.* New York: Houghton-Mifflin. http://www.twodollarsaday.com/.

16. Robin Smith, Susan Popkin, Taz George, and Jennifer Comey. 2015. "What Happens to Housing Assistance Leavers?" *Cityscape* 17(3): 213–244. https://www.huduser.gov/portal/periodicals/cityscpe/vol17num3/article10.html.

Bibliography

Adams, Gina, and Lisa Dubay. 2014. *Exploring Instability and Children's Well-Being: Insights from a Dialogue among Practitioners, Policymakers, and Researchers*. Washington, DC: The Urban Institute. http://www.urban.org/publications/413185.html.

Beider, Harris, Diane K. Levy, and Susan J. Popkin. 2009. *Community Revitalization in the United States and the United Kingdom*. Washington, DC: The Urban Institute. http://www.urban.org/research/publication/community-revitalization-united-states-and-united-kingdom.

Bennet, Larry, Janet L. Smith, and Patricia A. Wright, eds. *Where Are Poor People to Live? Transforming Public Housing Developments*. Armonk, NY: M.E. Sharpe.

Bloom, Howard, James Riccio, and Nandita Verma. 2005. *Promoting Work in Public Housing: The Effectiveness of Jobs Plus*. New York: MDRC. http://www.mdrc.org/publication/promoting-work-public-housing.

Boston, Thomas D. 2009. *Public Housing Transformation and Family Self-Sufficiency: A Case Study of Chicago and Atlanta Housing Authorities*. Working Paper draft. Author.

Briggs, Xavier de Souza, and Peter Dreier. 2008. "Memphis Murder Mystery? No, Just Mistaken Identity. *Shelterforce*, Posted July 22, 2008. http://www.shelterforce.org/article/special/1043.

Briggs, Xavier de Souza, Susan J. Popkin, and John Goering. 2010. *Moving to Opportunity: The Story of an American Experiment to Fight Ghetto Poverty*. Oxford: Oxford University Press.

Buron, Larry, Christopher Hayes, and Chantal Hailey. 2013. An Improved Living Environment, but ... Long-Term Outcomes for CHA Residents, Brief No. 3. Washington, DC: The Urban Institute. http://www.urban.org/research/publication/improved-living-environment.

Buron, Larry, Susan Popkin, Diane Levy, Laura Harris, and Jill Khadduri. 2002. *The HOPE VI Resident Tracking Study: A Snapshot of the Current Living Situation of*

Original Residents from Eight Sites. Washington, DC: The Urban Institute. http://www.urban.org/publications/410591.html.

Chaskin, Robert J., and Mark L. Joseph. 2015. *Integrating the Inner-City: The Promise and Perils of Mixed-Income Public Housing Transformation*. Chicago: University of Chicago Press.

Chetty, Raj, Nathaniel Hendren, and Lawrence F. Katz. 2015. *The Effects of Exposure to Better Neighborhood Environments on Children: New Evidence from the Moving to Opportunity Experiment*. Cambridge: National Bureau of Economic Research. http://www.equality-of-opportunity.org/images/mto_paper.pdf.

Chicago Housing Authority. 2000. *Plan for Transformation, January 6, 2000*. Chicago: Chicago Housing Authority. http://www.thecha.org/documents/?CategoryId=41&pg=2.

Cisneros, Henry G., and Lora Engdahl, eds. 2009. *From Despair to Hope: HOPE VI and the New Promise of Public Housing in American Cities*. Washington, DC: The Brookings Institution.

Comey, Jennifer, Susan J. Popkin, and Kaitlin Franks. 2012. "MTO: A Successful Housing Intervention." *Cityscape* 14(2): 87–107.

Cunningham, Mary K., Susan J. Popkin, Erin B. Godfrey, Beata A. Bednarz, Janet L. Smith, Anne Knepler, and Doug Schenkelberg. 2001. *CHAC Mobility Program: Interim Assessment*. Washington, DC: The Urban Institute. http://www.urban.org/research/publication/chac-mobility-program-assessment.

Dumke, Mitch. 2011 "A Neighborhood's Steady Decline." *New York Times*, April 28. http://www.nytimes.com/2011/04/29/us/29cncguns.html.

Edelman, Peter, Harry Holzer, and Paul Offner. 2006. *Reconnecting Disadvantaged Young Men*. Washington, DC: Urban Institute Press.

Edin, Kathryn J., and H. Luke Shaefer. 2015. *$2 A Day: Living on Almost Nothing in America*. New York: Houghton-Mifflin. http://www.twodollarsaday.com/.

Fanton, Jonathan. 2010. "Foreword." *Housing Policy Debate* 20(1): 5–6.

Fosburg, Linda B., Susan J. Popkin, and Gretchen P. Locke. 1996. *Historical and Baseline Assessment of HOPE VI Program: Volume 1: Cross-Site Report*. Washington, DC: U.S. Department of Housing and Urban Development.

Gallagher, Megan Gallagher. 2010. CHA Transformation: Children and Youth. CHA Families and the Plan for Transformation, Brief No. 4. Washington, DC: The Urban Institute. http://www.urban.org/research/publication/cha-transformation-children-and-youth.

Garbarino, James, Kathleen Kostelny, and Nancy Dubrow. 1991. *No Place to Be a Child: Growing Up in a War Zone*. New York: Lexington Books.

Gillespie, Sarah, and Susan J. Popkin. 2015. *Building Housing Authority Capacity for Better Resident Services*. Washington, DC: The Urban Institute. http://www.urban.org/research/publication/building-public-housing-authority-capacity-better-resident-services.

Goetz, Edward G. 2013. *New Deal Ruins: Race, Economic Justice, and Public Housing Policy*. Ithaca, NY: Cornell University Press.

Grossman, Kate. 2001. "CHA Families Still Stuck in the Projects." *Chicago Sun-Times*, July 11, 1.

Hailey, Chantal, and Megan Gallagher. 2013. Chronic Violence: Beyond the Developments. Long-Term Outcomes for CHA Families, Brief No. 5. Washington, DC: The Urban Institute. http://www.urban.org/research/publication/chronic-violence-beyond-developments.

Hailey, Chantal, and Priya Saxena. 2013. HOST: Helping Families, Building Community. HOST Brief No. 5. Washington, DC: The Urban Institute. http://www.urban.org/sites/default/files/alfresco/publication-pdfs/412952-HOST-Helping-Families-Building-Communities.pdf.

Hayes, Christopher, Graham McDonald, Susan Popkin, Leah Hendey, and Allison Stolte. 2013. "Public Housing Transformation and Crime: Are Relocatees More Likely to be Offenders or Victims?" *Cityscape* 15(3): 9–35.

Hendey, Leah, George C. Galster, Susan J. Popkin, and Chris Hayes. 2015. "Housing Choice Voucher Holders and Neighborhood Crime: A Dynamic Panel Analysis." *Urban Affairs Review.* http://uar.sagepub.com/content/early/2015/06/30/1078087415591348.full.pdf+html.

Herr, Toby, and Susan Wagner. 2009. "Labor Economics versus Barriers to Work versus Human Development: Finding the Right Lens for Looking at Labor Force Attachment." In Margery A. Turner, Susan J. Popkin, and Lynette Rawlings, *Public Housing and the Legacy of Segregation.* Washington, DC: Urban Institute Press, 221–236.

Hirsch. Arnold R. 1998. *Making the Second Ghetto*, 2nd ed. Chicago: University of Chicago Press.

Holin, Mary J., Larry F. Buron, and Michael Baker. 2003. *Interim Assessment of the HOPE VI Program: Case Studies.* Bethesda, MD: Abt Associates.

Hooven, Carole, Paula Nurius, Patricia LoganGreene, and Elaine Thompson. 2012. "Childhood Violence Exposure: Cumulative and Specific Effects on Adult Mental Health." *Journal of Family Violence* 27(6): 511–522.

Hunt, D. Bradford. 2010. *Blueprint for Disaster: The Unraveling of Chicago Public Housing.* Chicago: University of Chicago Press.

Jacob, Brian A. 2004. "Public Housing Vouchers, and Student Achievement: Evidence from Public Housing Demolitions in Chicago." *American Economic Review* 94(1) (Mar): 233–258.

Joint Center on Housing Studies Harvard University. 2015. *America's Rental Housing—Evolving Markets and Needs.* Boston: Harvard University. http://www.jchs.harvard.edu/sites/jchs.harvard.edu/files/ahr2013_01-intro.pdf.

Kotlowitz, Alex. 1991. *There Are No Children Here: The Story of Two Boys Growing Up in the Other America.* New York: Doubleday.

Levy. Diane K. 2010. The Limits of Relocation: Employment and Family Well-Being among Former Madden/Wells Residents. CHA Families and the Plan for Transformation, Brief No. 6. http://www.urban.org/sites/default/files/alfresco/publication-pdfs/412186-The-Limits-of-Relocation-Employment-and-Family-Well-Being-among-Former-Madden-Wells-Residents.pdf.

Levy, Diane K., and Megan Gallagher. 2006. *HOPE VI and Neighborhood Revitalization.* A Report to the MacArthur Foundation. Washington, DC: The Urban Institute. http://www.urban.org/research/publication/hope-vi-and-neighborhood-revitalization.

Manjarrez, Carlos A., Susan J. Popkin, and Elizabeth Guernsey. 2007. Poor Health: Adding Insult to Injury for HOPE VI Families. HOPE VI: Where Do We Go from Here? Brief 5. Washington, DC: The Urban Institute. http://www.urban.org/projects/hopevi/index.cfm.

Massey, Douglas S. and Nancy A. Denton. 1998. *American Apartheid: Segregation and the Making of the Underclass*. Cambridge, MA: Harvard University Press.

McDaniel, Marla S. Darius Tandon, Caroline Heller, Gina Adams, and Susan J. Popkin. 2015. *Addressing Parents' Mental Health Needs in Home Visiting Services in Public Housing*. Washington, DC: The Urban Institute. http://www.urban.org/research/publication/addressing-parents-mental-health-home-visiting-services-public-housing.

Medina, Jennifer. 2011. "Subsidies and Suspicion." *New York Times*, August 11. http://www.nytimes.com/2011/08/11/us/11housing.html?_r=2&src=me&ref=us; Joint Center on Housing Studies Harvard University. 2015. *America's Rental Housing—Evolving Markets and Needs*. Boston: Harvard University. http://www.jchs.harvard.edu/sites/jchs.harvard.edu/files/ahr2013_01-intro.pdf.

Murray, Brittany, Elsa Falkenburger, and Priya Saxena. 2015. *Data Walks: An Innovative Way to Share Data with Communities*. Washington, DC: The Urban Institute. http://www.urban.org/research/publication/data-walks-innovative-way-share-data-communities.

National Commission on Severely Distressed Public Housing (U.S.). 1993. *The Final Report of the National Commission on Severely Distressed Public Housing: A Report to the Congress and the Secretary of Housing and Urban Development*. Washington, DC: The Commission: For sale by the U.S. G.P.O., Supt. of Docs.

National Housing Law Project. 2002. *False Hope: A Critical Assessment of the HOPE VI Public Housing Redevelopment Program*. Washington, DC: Center for Community Change.

Popkin, Susan J. 1991. "Welfare: Views from the Bottom." *Social Problems* 37(1): 64–79.

Popkin, Susan J. 1999. "No Simple Solutions for Housing the Poor." *Chicago Tribune* May 30. http://articles.chicagotribune.com/1999-05-30/news/9905300119_1_landlords-chicago-housing-authority-cha.

Popkin, Susan J. 2006. "No Simple Solutions: Housing CHA's Most Vulnerable Families." *Journal of Law and Social Policy* 1(1): 148–166. http://www.law.northwestern.edu/journals/njlsp/v1/n1/index.html.

Popkin, Susan J. 2010. "A Glass Half-Empty: Public Housing Families in Transition." *Housing Policy Debate* 20(1): 42–62.

Popkin, J. Susan J. Larry Buron, Diane K. Levy, and Mary K. Cunningham. 2000. "The Gautreaux Legacy: What Might Mixed-Income and Dispersal Strategies Mean for the Poorest Public Housing Tenants?" *Housing Policy Debate* 11(4): 911–942.

Popkin, Susan J., and Mary K. Cunningham. 2000. *Searching for Rental Housing with Section 8 in Chicago*. Washington, DC: The Urban Institute. http://www.urban.org/research/publication/searching-rental-housing-section-8-chicago-region.

Popkin, Susan J., and Mary K. Cunningham. 2002. *CHA Relocation and Mobility Counseling Assessment Final Report*. Report prepared by the Urban Institute for the John D. and Catherine T. MacArthur Foundation. Washington, DC: The Urban Institute.

Popkin, Susan J., and Mary K. Cunningham. 2005. "Demolition and Struggle: Public Housing Transformation in Chicago and the Challenges for Residents" in Xavier de Souza Briggs (ed), *Housing Race and Regionalism: Re-thinking the Geography of Race in America.* Washington, DC: Brookings.

Popkin, Susan J., Mary K. Cunningham, and Martha Burt. 2005. "Public Housing Transformation and the Hard to House." *Housing Policy Debate* 16(1): 1–24.

Popkin, Susan J., and Elizabeth Davies. 2013. Improving the Lives of Public Housing's Most Vulnerable Families. Long-Term Outcomes for CHA Residents, Brief No. 4. Washington, DC: The Urban Institute. http://www.urban.org/publications/412763. html.

Popkin, Susan J., Megan Gallagher, Chantal Hailey, Elizabeth Davies, Larry Buron, and Christopher Hayes. 2013. CHA Residents and the Plan for Transformation. Long-Term Outcomes for CHA Residents, Brief No. 2. Washington, DC: The Urban Institute. http://www.urban.org/publications/412761.html.

Popkin, Susan J., and Liza Getsinger. 2010. Reaching the Next Generation: The Crisis for CHA's Youth. Supporting Vulnerable Public Housing Families, Brief No. 6. Washington, DC: The Urban Institute. http://www.urban.org/research/publication/reaching-next-generation-crisis-chas-youth.

Popkin, Susan J., Victoria E. Gwiasda, Dennis P. Rosenbaum, Lynn M. Olson, and F. Larry. Buron. 2000. *The Hidden War: Crime and the Tragedy of Public Housing in Chicago.* New Brunswick, NJ: Rutgers University Press.

Popkin, Susan. J., Chantal Hailey, Janine Zweig, Nan Astone, Reed Jordan, Leah Gordon, and Jay Silverman. 2016. "Coercive Sexual Environments: Exploring the Linkages to Mental Health in Public Housing." *Cityscape* 18(1): 165–182.

Popkin, Susan J., Bruce Katz, Mary K. Cunningham, Karen D. Brown, Jeremy Gustafson, and Margery Austin Turner. 2004. *A Decade of HOPE VI: Research Findings and Policy Challenges.* Washington, DC: The Urban Institute. http://www.urban.org/research/publication/decade-hope-vi.

Popkin, Susan J., Tama Leventhal, and Gretchen Weissman. 2010. "Girls in the 'Hood: How Safety Affects the Life Chances of Low-Income Girls." *Urban Affairs Review* 45(6): 715–774.

Popkin, Susan J., Diane K. Levy, and Larry Buron. 2009. "Has HOPE VI Transformed Residents' Lives? New Evidence from the HOPE VI Panel Study." *Housing Studies* 24(4): 477–502.

Popkin, Susan J, Diane K. Levy, Laura E. Harris, Jennifer Comey, Mary K. Cunningham, and Larry F. Buron. 2002. *HOPE VI Panel Study: Baseline Report.* Washington, DC: The Urban Institute.

Popkin, Susan, J., Diane K. Levy, Laura E. Harris, Jennifer Comey, Mary K. Cunningham, and Larry Buron. 2004. "The HOPE VI Program: What about the Residents?" *Housing Policy Debate*, 15(2): 385–414.

Popkin, Susan J., and Marla McDaniel. 2013. HOST: Can Public Housing Be a Platform for Change. HOST Working Paper. Washington, DC: The Urban Institute. http://www.urban.org/UploadedPDF/412965-host-can-public-housing.pdf.

Popkin, Susan J., Michael J. Rich, Leah Hendey, Christopher Hayes, and Joseph Parilla. 2012. *Public Housing Transformation and Crime: Making the Case for Responsible Relocation.* Washington, DC: The Urban Institute. http://www.urban.org/research/publication/public-housing-transformation-and-crime-making-case-responsible-relocation.

Popkin, Susan J., Michael J. Rich, Leah Hendey, Christopher Hayes, Joseph Parilla, and George Galster. 2012. "Public Housing Transformation and Crime: Making the Case for Responsible Relocation." *Cityscape* 14(3): 137–160. http://www.huduser.org/portal/periodicals/cityscpe/vol14num3/Cityscape_Nov2012_pub_house_trans.pdf.

Popkin, Susan J., Molly M. Scott, Joe Parilla, Elsa Falkenburger, and Shinwon Kyung. 2012. Planning the Housing Opportunities and Services Together Demonstration. HOST Brief No. 1. Washington, DC: The Urban Institute. http://www.urban.org/research/publication/planning-housing-opportunity-and-services-together-demonstration.

Popkin, Susan J., Brett Theodos, Liza Getsinger, and Joe Parilla. 2010. An Overview of the Chicago Family Case Management Demonstration. Supporting Vulnerable Public Housing Families, Brief No. 1. Washington, DC: The Urban Institute. http://www.urban.org/publications/412254.html.

Popkin, Susan J., Brett Theodos, Caterina Roman, and Elizabeth Guernsey. 2008. *The Chicago Family Case Management Demonstration: Developing a New Model for Serving "Hard to House" Public Housing Families.* Washington, DC: The Urban Institute. http://www.urban.org/publications/411708.html.

Price, David, and Susan J. Popkin. 2010. The Health Crisis for CHA Families. CHA Families and the Plan for Transformation, Brief No. 5. Washington, DC: The Urban Institute. http://www.urban.org/publications/412184.html.

Roman, Caterina Gouvis, and Carly Knight. 2009. *An Examination of the Social and Physical Environment of Public Housing Residents in Two Chicago Developments in Transition.* Washington, DC: The Urban Institute. http://www.urban.org/research/publication/examination-social-and-physical-environment-public-housing-residents-two-chicago-developments-transition.

Rosin, Hanna. 2008. "American Murder Mystery." *The Atlantic Monthly* 302(1): 40–54.

Rubinowitz, Leonard S., and James D. Rosenbaum. 2000. *Crossing the Class and Color Lines: From Public Housing to White Suburbia.* Chicago: University of Chicago Press.

Sacks, Vanessa, David Murphey, and Kristen Moore. 2014. Adverse Childhood Experiences: National and State-Level Prevalence. Research Brief 2014-28. Washington, DC: ChildTrends. http://www.childtrends.org/wp-content/uploads/2014/07/Brief-adverse-childhood-experiences_FINAL.pdf.

Sampson, Robert J. 2012. *Great American City: Chicago and the Enduring Neighborhood Effect.* Chicago, University of Chicago Press.

Sandel, Megan, 2014. "Can the Housing Vaccine Help a Community? Thinking from People to Populations." Children's Health Watch, Posted November 4, 2014. http://www.childrenshealthwatch.org/2014/11/can-housing-vaccine-help-community-thinking-people-populations/.

Scanlon, Edward, and Kevin Devine. 2001. "Residential Mobility and Youth Well-Being: Research, Policy, and Practice Issues." *Journal of Sociology and Social Welfare* 28(1): 119–138.

Scott, Molly M., Susan J. Popkin, Marla McDaniel, Priya Saxena, and Reed Jordan. 2013. Serving HOST Families: The Challenges to Overcome. Housing Opportunities and Services Together, Brief No. 3. Washington, DC: The Urban Institute. http://www.urban.org/research/publication/serving-host-families-challenges-overcome.

Scott, Molly M., Susan J. Popkin, and Priya Saxena. 2016. *Making a Two-Generation Approach Work in the Real World: Lessons from the HOST Demonstration.* Washington, DC: The Urban Institute. http://www.urban.org/research/publication/making-two-generation-model-work-real-world.

Smith, Robin, Susan Popkin, Taz George, and Jennifer Comey. 2015. "What Happens to Housing Assistance Leavers?" *Cityscape* 17(3): 213–244. https://www.huduser.gov/portal/periodicals/cityscpe/vol17num3/article10.html.

Sullivan, Thomas P. 2003. *Independent Monitor's Report No. 5 to the Chicago Housing Authority and the Central Advisory Council.* Chicago: Author.

Theodos, Brett, Susan J. Popkin, Joe Parilla, and Liza Getsinger. 2012. "The Challenge of Targeting Services: A Typology of Public Housing Residents," *Social Service Review* 86(3): 517–544.

Turner, Margery A., Peter Edelman, Erika Poethig, and Laudan Aron. 2014. *Tackling Persistent Poverty in Distressed Urban Neighborhoods.* Washington, DC: The Urban Institute. http://www.urban.org/research/publication/tackling-persistent-poverty-distressed-urban-neighborhoods.

Turner, Margery A., and G. Thomas Kingsley. 2008. *Federal Programs for Addressing Low-Income Housing Needs.* Washington, DC: The Urban Institute. http://www.urban.org/research/publication/federal-programs-addressing-low-income-housing-needs.

Turner, Margery A., Susan J. Popkin, and Lynette Rawlings. 2009. *Public Housing Transformation: The Legacy of Segregation.* Washington, DC: Urban Institute Press.

Vale, Lawrence. 2013. *Purging the Poorest: Public Housing and the Design Politics of Twice-Cleared Communities.* Chicago: University of Chicago Press.

Venkatesh, Sudhir A. 2002. *American Project: The Rise and Fall of a Modern Ghetto.* Cambridge, MA: Harvard University Press.

Venkatesh, Sudhir A, Isil Celimli, Douglas Miller, Alexandra Murphy, and Beauty Turner. 2004. *Chicago Public Housing Transformation: A Research Report.* Center for Urban Research and Policy Working Paper. New York, NY: Columbia University. http://www.columbia.edu/cu/curp/publications2/PH_Transformation_Report.pdf.

Wilen, Willam P., and Rajesh D. Nayak. 2006. "Relocated Public Housing Residents Have Little Hope of Returning: Work Requirements for Mixed-Income Public Housing Developments." In Larry Bennet, Janet L. Smith, and Patricia A. Wright (eds.). *Where are Poor People to Live? Transforming Public Housing Developments.* Armonk, NY: M.E. Sharpe: 216–238.

Wilson, William Julius. 2012. *The Truly Disadvantaged: The Inner-City, the Underclass, and Public Policy. Second Edition.* Chicago: University of Chicago Press.

Index

Note: Italicized page numbers indicate tables and figures.

About the Author

Susan J. Popkin is both Director of The Urban Institute's Program on Neighborhoods and Youth Development and a Senior Fellow in the Metropolitan Housing and Communities Policy Center. A nationally-recognized expert on assisted housing and mobility, Dr. Popkin directs a research program that focuses on the ways neighborhood environments affect outcomes for youth, and in conducting evaluations of complex community-based interventions. Current projects include the multi-site HOST demonstration, which is testing strategies for using housing as a platform for two-generation service models; Teens and Food Insecurity, a partnership with Feeding America to address the link between hunger and risky behavior; Promoting Adolescent Sexual Health and Safety, a community-based effort to develop a curriculum to reduce the impact of coercive sexual environments on young girls; and the evaluation of the Annie E. Casey Foundation's Family Centered Community Change Initiative. This work builds on her research on how the radical changes in housing policy over the past twenty years have affected the lives of the most vulnerable public and assisted housing families, including two decades of research on public housing transformation in Chicago, the HOPE VI Panel Study, the first large-scale, systematic look at outcomes for families involuntarily relocated from public housing; the Chicago Family Case Management Demonstration, which tested the impact and cost-effectiveness of intensive services for the most troubled public housing residents; the Three City Study of Moving to Opportunity; and the analysis of housing and mobility outcomes for the MTO Final Evaluation.

In addition to her expertise on housing policy, Dr. Popkin is an expert on formative evaluation using the Plan-Do-Study-Act (PDSA) model, as well as an expert on qualitative research methods, including in-depth interviews with low-income families, focus groups, ethnographic observations, and administrative interviews. Her particular expertise is in integrating these methods into large, multi-method projects. Dr. Popkin is the sole author of this book; coauthor of the award-winning *Moving To Opportunity: The Story of an American Experiment to Fight Ghetto Poverty*; lead author for *The Hidden War: Crime and the Tragedy of Public Housing in Chicago*; and coauthor of *Public Housing Transformation: The Legacy of Segregation*. Dr. Popkin is also the author of numerous papers and book chapters on housing and poverty-related issues.